Introducing The Holistic Emotional Makeover Success System

Fast Inner Healing for Happy, Healthy & Successful Living!

Kathleen Fors

This book is intended to enhance and promote emotional, physical, spiritual, and professional wellness. Sharing stories and recommendations is not intended to address a specific medical or mental diagnosis. Kathleen Fors is NOT a licensed therapist or healthcare provider.

This book does NOT diagnose or treat medical illnesses, diseases, or psychological disorders. It is not a substitute for diagnosis and treatment by a licensed physician, psychiatrist, or psychologist.

This book does not recommend that anyone discontinue any treatment or prescriptions prescribed by a licensed health care provider.

The person reading this book understands and agrees that they are fully responsible for their physical, mental, and emotional well-being, including choices and decisions made during and after reading this book.

This book does not make any promises or guarantees to the reader.

If a person has a drug or alcohol addiction, a prospective client must first be in an on-site rehab program.

ISBN: 979-8-9885650-8-6

Contents

This book is dedicated to those seeking and committed to feeling good, happy, healthy, and living a successful life.

Foreword

When you've tried a multitude of different things to heal yourself, you can start to feel hopeless. I told myself there wasn't anything dramatically wrong in my life, but I had a lot of small things sabotaging me from feeling happy or successful in anything. For example, I ate ice cream to soothe my emotions and felt powerless to stop. Then, there was an accident where I totaled my car. Even though I wasn't injured, I was experiencing flashbacks and an intense fear of driving.

I tried traditional therapy but could never find a therapist that made a difference. Kathleen Fors promised not only healing but fast healing. I was skeptical about how my most deep-seated issues could be resolved in moments, especially after all the programs I had tried. But then I experienced mountains of junk leaving my head and my subconscious. Limiting beliefs just going poof when the light was held up to them. There was so much clearing in our sessions, I felt like I was reaching for any little hiccup to get rid of. It was a giddy feeling, like *what can we clear out next?*

At first, I didn't trust that the issues were really cleared. I waited for the proverbial other shoe to drop, expecting the problems to come back. Then, week after week passed, and I was no longer afraid to drive. Most incredibly, I no longer crave ice cream. Even when my kids are screaming, I no longer need to run to food. Now, I have a pleasant and easy relationship with ice cream. I can choose whether it's something I feel like eating or not. I never thought I would ever experience that!

This book will introduce you to Kathleen's philosophy of healing. You will read her intense history and how she developed a system that could heal her. The transformation in her life is staggering, and the transformation that has occurred in my life has given me the freedom to be me, feel good about myself, and be inspired, all at the same time with ease.

Once you learn about the Holistic Emotional Makeover Success System™ (HEMSS), I highly encourage you to work with Kathleen one-on-one or take her training program. No matter where you are stuck in your life, she can help.

-Carolyn Choate

Chapter One

Introduction: Why Talking Isn't Enough

> If you want to find out the secrets of the Universe, think in terms of energy, frequency, and vibration. – **Nikola Tesla**

I have taken hundreds of personal development classes, read dozens of books, gone through four coaching programs conducted by high-level professionals, worked with nine coaches, eight healers, and four therapists, and learned four healing modalities. Yes, there is a ton of great information and certified practitioners worldwide.

However, I have learned that it doesn't matter how much information you know; if you have "sabotaging beliefs" operating, they can stop you from feeling good about yourself, being happy, healthy, and living a successful life. Your belief system, conscious and unconscious, controls your feelings, thoughts, thinking, behavior, actions, and results.

When I started my healing process over 40 years ago, I was at the bottom of David R. Hawkins's Ladder of Consciousness. I strongly recommend reading his book, *Power vs. Force*. Dr. Hawkins shows how healing takes place by climbing up the consciousness ladder. I was filled with shame, guilt, sadness, and fear. These emotions are all 100 points or lower on the ladder. I was on the low end because of my childhood trauma. More information did not help me feel better about myself.

When children experience trauma, they make up sabotaging beliefs about themselves and their lives that can control their feelings, thinking, and behavior as adults.

Here is a simple explanation of how our internal beliefs make up the programming that runs our lives.

The binary system used by computers was designed after human beings. Our success in life is programmed by thousands of tiny switches deep within us that are either "on" or "off" for beliefs regarding self, money, career, relationships, health, happiness, etc. This is each person's programming.

There are dozens of books and speakers talking about the power of beliefs. Napoleon Hill's 1954 classic, *Think and Grow Rich*, has launched many people on the path to their success. Henry Ford stated, "If you believe you can or can't, you're right." The film *The Secret* made the Law of Attraction a household term.

This is how it works: Our beliefs—both conscious and unconscious—determine our feelings, thoughts, thinking, behavior, actions, and results. Our belief system is formed by age seven or eight; however, an upsetting or traumatic incident at any age can significantly negatively impact us, hold us back, cause frustration, fear, doubt, or insecurities, and create health problems.

When limiting core beliefs are identified and cleared, those things we want to be, do, and have come naturally without effort or strain. This is the basis of my unique Holistic Emotional Makeover Success System™ (HEMSS). Our internal belief programming gets changed, so instead of trying to manage our behavior, we just feel differently, think differently, and act differently. This is a massive distinction compared to traditional coaching and therapy. And since everything is energy, frequency, and vibration, we automatically attract more positive people and circumstances into our lives when our internal belief programming gets upgraded. When we change our beliefs, we change our life.

However, many sabotaging beliefs are unconscious and illogical, making them extremely difficult to identify. And even if the limiting beliefs are identified, most mental health practitioners, coaches, therapists, and even some healers do not have the training and skill set to clear them. This significant distinction is one of the main differences that separates my unique HEMSS from all the other transformation programs that I have gone through or heard about.

Once I finally understood the foundational clearing work needed, I developed the HEMSS to help people heal quickly from all kinds of challenges. It does not have to take years or decades to reach emotional and physical good health, good relationships, and professional goals.

The HEMSS is a spiritual-based program, with the healing done by the "Creator of All That Is," "Greater Field of Life," or whatever name you'd like to use. There are well over one hundred names used to describe "God." The HEMSS provides what is optimal to clear, using muscle testing and uncovering the true root of the sabotaging beliefs, then connects with the "Creator of All That Is" to do the healing.

I offer a one-on-one program of twelve sessions for those who want fast healing.

For those who want to learn the HEMSS, I intend to pass on all the information I have learned and developed over the past 30 years so healers, life coaches, and wellness practitioners can help their clients significantly faster. I will describe the HEMSS training later in the book.

Chapter Two

Good Emotional Health

What is Good Emotional Health?

You have good emotional health when you feel good about yourself and your life. Things don't have to be perfect; life has ups and downs, but most of the time, you feel peaceful, confident, whole, and complete, like nothing is missing. You know you have value and worth without doing anything to prove it. You communicate in a healthy way and have good boundaries. Most of the time, you feel happy and grateful and are kind to yourself and others without self-sacrifice. You can ask for what you want without expectations. You are in touch with your emotions without stuffing them down and know how to process the ones that don't feel good. You are conscious of your behavior, can be self-reflective, and take responsibility for your part in an upset. And you are living your purpose.

Why is Good Emotional Health Critical?

A person's emotional health impacts every area of their life. It affects their physical health, quality of life, relationships, family, and career. Suppose you don't have good emotional health. In that case, you might feel out of control, overwhelmed with unwanted emotions, exhausted, depressed, stressed, and not know what to do to solve your problems. You might be on the verge of getting a divorce, have work challenges, health issues, addictions, or other challenges. The bottom line is that you are unhappy, and your life isn't working the way you want.

When should people start searching for someone to help them improve their Emotional Health?

It is optimal for people to start searching for someone to help them when they feel anxious, overwhelmed, depressed, and their life isn't working, or simply because they don't feel good about themselves and their lives. There are statements at the end of the book that you can use to get more clarity.

Who is responsible for your Emotional Health?

Until you are an adult, your parents are responsible for your emotional health. And whether they do a good or poor job of raising you doesn't matter once you are an adult. Of course, we'd all like to blame our parents for our problems, but that will not help us live happier lives. That will only make things worse. As an adult, we must take responsibility for our own lives. And when we have problems, we must be willing to reflect on our thinking, emotions, and behavior and take responsibility for our part.

Where can I get help to improve my Emotional Health?

Many healing practitioners, coaches, and therapists offer their services to help. I went to more than three dozen myself. They were kind and knowledgeable, but if you have childhood trauma, which everyone has even when raised in a healthy family, you need more than just talking to someone. I suggest powerful healing work.

Later in this book, I will provide questions you can ask a professional you are considering hiring to find out how much they can help you.

Throughout this book, I provide "Life Learning Points," some elementary and some profound. I suggest you note them and see if they apply to your life (and your clients if you are a practitioner).

When a person feels overwhelmed with life and has an addiction, it is often someone’s best attempt to cope when they can’t see other options. The best thing to do is heal their childhood trauma, anger, anxiety, depression, despair, and victim beliefs and behavior. This is the foundation of Kathleen's revolutionary Holistic Emotional Makeover Success System™ (HEMSS), which produces permanent empowering results quickly.

Chapter Three

My Story

How early childhood experiences shaped my life.

My story will share what I have done over the past 40 years to go from being a victim and suffering to being and feeling whole and complete and having a great life.

Before I share my story, I want you to know I don't want you to feel bad for me. This is because I now live a magical life beyond my wildest imagination. Every challenge I have experienced provided me with information I could incorporate into my coaching and healing practice. Without these experiences, I could not have developed the powerful HEMSS. Also, I am at peace with my parents, who passed on many years ago. I forgive them, and I know they did the best they could with the upbringing they experienced. I also forgive my brother and myself.

As an adult, I got along well with my parents, and I feel I was a respectful, caring daughter, calling and visiting them regularly and supporting them in their later years.

No matter what you have been through, you can be hopeful for a better future without taking years or decades. I will share many of my struggles and how, now, at 76 years young, I feel healthy and fit, and I am living my dreams of playing competitive tennis, golf, pickleball, and winning medals. And guess what? I got married for the first at 71 to a fantastic man who is my partner in all my sports activities. A man with great humor, makes me laugh and shares my values.

Most of my life has felt like a struggle. The first traumatic experience that I remember was at age three. My mother was the type who was strict and did not demonstrate affection. I remember we were in the kitchen, and I wanted to be picked up. My mother was probably baking bread, which she often did, and refused to pick me up, so I threw myself on the floor and had a tantrum. What else could a three-year-old think up?

My mother responded by spanking me and telling me to "stop crying, or she would give me something to cry about," a prevalent mantra in those days. I ran and hid in the closet in my bedroom, stomped my feet, hit my fists against the wall, and cried – "I hate you, I hate you, I hate you!" Then I decided to run away.

As I marched down the country road in front of our house, an eighteen-wheeler sped by and almost knocked me down. This was scary, and in that instant, my spirit was broken. I thought, "I am not big enough to care for myself. I need my mother's attention to survive. I need to be taken care of." I slithered back into the house, feeling shame. I decided right then I would be a "good little girl," not asking for anything or showing any anger because that was dangerous. I would need to stuff down all of my feelings. These beliefs were my plan to survive: "Do what mommy wants me to do to get the attention and affection I deeply desire and (think) I need to survive."

Out of this traumatic incident, I created dozens of sabotaging beliefs (many true in this situation) that controlled my life and resulted in me being a victim. The most damaging belief was, "I can't take care of myself." This showed up everywhere in my life for the next 60 years.

Life Learning Point:

One childhood trauma can break a child. Then, they might spend the rest of their life feeling broken, operating from sabotaging beliefs they created.

***

I did what I was told and didn't ask for anything. I tried to be perfect and please my mother so she wouldn't get angry and reject me. Rejection felt like death. Other people's anger meant danger, too. My feelings got shut down. I felt unsafe saying "no" to my mother because she might get angry and hit me. I didn't have healthy boundaries and walked around on eggshells, trying not to disturb the dragon.

These beliefs were deeply ingrained and controlled my behavior in every area of my life. Being unable to say "no" and stand up for myself and fearing other people's anger was very disempowering and caused me all sorts of problems and abuse as a child and as an adult.

Later, I discovered childhood trauma is highly toxic for adults. When children cannot express their emotions, and they push them down or numb them out, it is very destructive to a person's mental and physical health. Studies show that childhood trauma that is not resolved can cause all sorts of health problems later on in life.

In my case, in my youth, I often got sore throats. In high school, I discovered I was overly sensitive when I had to quit the swim team because my skin broke out in hives from the chlorine. In my 40s, I went to the chiropractor at least 4 – 6 times yearly for neck pain. Every time I've had to take an antibiotic, I broke out in red hives. When I was sick with inflammation, I got a flu shot and had a reaction. My body was overly sensitive.

Once, when I was napping at age three or four, my mother came into my bedroom and found me touching my privates. Of course, I knew nothing about it, but my mother scolded me anyway and told me never to touch myself again. This incident caused me confusion, embarrassment, guilt, and shame about my sexual body parts.

Another time, when I was maybe 7 or 8 years old, I must have done something very upsetting because my mother hit me with a wooden hanger until it broke. It was shocking to me and further engrained my sabotaging beliefs and feelings of being unsafe and unworthy.

When I was in 7th grade, I was invited to a Halloween party. Moments before we left the house, my mother pulled a full-length bunny suit out of a storage drawer and told me to put it on. Obeying, I did. Walking up the walkway to the party, I felt mortified. I knocked on the door, and when it opened, a group of fellow students started howling with laughter. None of them were wearing costumes. At that moment, I wanted to die; I was so embarrassed. Thankfully, the party host took me quickly into her bedroom and gave me some clothes to wear. But for the next two years in school, I tried to be invisible.

When I was fifteen and sixteen, If I didn't do what my mother wanted, she would yell, "You are such a baby! Why can't you be like so-and-so's daughter." This happened often until so-and-so's daughter got pregnant in her senior year.

My mother's love was very conditional. She was controlling and got angry quickly. These were characteristics her parents had. She grew up in Red Lodge,

Montana, a Finnish community. Her parents worked extremely hard, as did most people. My mother was born in 1920. Her family had a farm just outside of town, a few miles away. They originally had to clear the land of rocks so they could farm it. They had milk cows, sterns for beef, chickens, and raised alfalfa. They survived the depression and were generous to feed people who were starving. If anyone walked out from town to the farm, my grandparents would always give them a meal. These strict, no-nonsense Finish people worked 12 – 14 hours daily except Sundays. They made bread and butter and sewed their clothes. They were homesteaders.

Even though my mother didn't like being treated harshly as a child, she carried many of her parents' characteristics with her when she got on a bus right out of high school and traveled to San Francisco.

So, that explains her behavior when I had a tantrum. She was just following the behavior that her mom would have taken.

Life Learning Point:

It is good to be self-reflective and notice what you dislike about your parents. Being around them 24/7 for the first 15 – 18 years of your life, a person often acquires undesirable characteristics that they dislike about their parents. The apple doesn't fall too far from the tree, as they say.

***

My mother was a great cook, and we were fed well. When I was growing up, we lived in the country with fig trees, vineyards, and alfalfa fields around. We had a cow, chickens, a steer, and a couple of horses. My mother milked the cow and made butter and bread. And every year or two, my dad would butcher a steer so we would have meat in the freezer.

My mother was well-known among our relatives for making the world's best pancakes. She wiped the egg whites and folded them into the homemade batter. Then, she boiled sugar water to make hot syrup. And sometimes, she would put an over-easy egg on top of the stack of pancakes. When my male cousins visited, they would eat stacks of pancakes. And until they all passed, they talked about the great memories of eating my mom's pancakes. We had a tiny kitchen, so my mother did all the cooking. Unfortunately, I never learned how to cook, a regret I have.

My mother sewed and made clothes for us, but I also got my older sister's hand-me-downs. To this day, I don't like to shop at second-hand or consignment stores.

Part of my problem growing up was that I didn't have anyone to talk to, and my parents weren't emotionally healthy. I don't remember having a personal conversation with my mother except once when I was 45. While visiting my parents' home in Fresno, I sobbed quietly in the guest bedroom because my boyfriend had just broken up with me. I was practicing feeling my emotions, which was something new for me. When my mother discovered me, she asked what was wrong, and I told her. She said: "Stop it right now. If Dad finds out, he will get upset; we can't have that!" That was the only time I remember being vulnerable and authentic with her, and it didn't go well. It felt hurtful and seemed like another message that supported my feelings of being unimportant, an underlying theme in my life.

When I was 9, my dad built a swimming pool in the backyard. I spent hours in the pool each day all summer long. How lucky was I?

One Christmas around that time, my parents told me they didn't have enough money to buy presents, which was disappointing and confusing. But at the last minute, they put a present under the tree for me, which made me hopeful. When I opened my gift, it contained socks and underwear, returning me to disappointment. This supported my limiting belief, "I am not worthy and deserving." And it added a new limiting belief, "Money is scarce and hard to get."

We also had horses, so in elementary school, my girlfriend, Candace, and I would ride bareback all over and sometimes down to the river a mile and a half away. One year, when I was about 12, I rode my pony, Babe, about 7 miles to ride in the annual Clovis Rodeo Parade. Riding alone, I remember being scared because Babe could sometimes be stubborn.

I was very blessed to have a great childhood and to experience many different things that most kids didn't. But under all these opportunities and blessings were feelings of being inferior and fearful and wondering what was wrong with me.

Even though my mother attended a one-room schoolhouse and her native language was Finnish, her English was excellent, and she could spell anything. No college, but my mother found a house for my dad's mother, who was in her 90s, to live in. It proved to be a good investment that helped them later on financially.

Unlike my mother, my dad had a degree in agriculture from the University of Davis, close to Sacramento. He was the youngest of 7 children. His parents, originally from Illinois, had moved to the Northern plains of Colorado and then to Fresno, California, where they bought a vineyard with three houses on the property. When my parents married, they eventually purchased 3 acres across the street and built a home.

My dad was a man who wanted to help everyone and bring all the relatives together. Despite my parents being on a very tight budget, my dad would invite his relatives to our home for major holidays. I always felt sorry for my mom as she never left the kitchen; she was always cooking. I remember having 35 – 40 relatives at our home on lots of holidays. Some camped out in our backyard, while others slept in our finished garage with four double beds.

My father was my source of affection, love, and security. When I was 7 or 8 years old, he would take me to his downtown office, and while walking down the street holding my hand, he would introduce me to everyone he knew and say hello to everyone we passed. He was super friendly, an excellent attribute for anyone to have. He was also very generous with people, always helping others whenever possible. He was likable.

Then, at nine years old, all those warm, safe, and loving feelings were gone forever. My mother had taken my brother, who was six years younger, to Montana to visit her dying father. My two sisters, five and a half and four years older, were out with their friends. I was left alone with my dad. One night, I woke in shock to find my dad in bed with me, sexually abusing me. I was traumatized, and I remember my spirit leaving my body and going up to the corner of the room. I didn't know what to think or do, except I was frightened and went numb.

After this incident, I had to start wearing glasses and had difficulty hearing. Reading and comprehension were challenging, and I felt like my whole brain got scrambled.

I now know I was experiencing the full-blown effects of PTSD.

I didn't dare share this information with my mother. I was afraid she would call me a liar and beat me. So, instead, I stuffed all my fear and confusion down and continued to be numb, walking around totally inauthentic and not present.

The effects of my trauma must have been evident to my teacher because I remember my dad taking me to the principal's office and me sitting on the bench in the back of the room. At the same time, my father made up excuses for me not functioning normally. My dad said, "Kathleen is just like me regarding tests; she blanks out."

The beliefs I created from this sexual abuse incident were highly destructive. Here are a few sabotaging beliefs I created: "Love cannot be trusted," "People who are supposed to love me will betray me," and "I can't feel safe with anyone." Having these beliefs as an adult, I always picked unavailable men. And most of the men I dated had just gotten divorced or broken up with a girlfriend. I treated these men special and nurtured them back to their confident selves, only to be rejected and dropped a year or two later.

After 40 years of working on myself, I now know I had many opposing beliefs operating simultaneously, which was crazy-making. On the one hand, I was needy with men, and on the other hand, I picked guys who were not available, a combination that equaled emotional pain.

Until I was 30, I had a significant learning disability. I couldn't understand what I read. I had to read a sentence three times before it made sense. I couldn't compose a sentence when I needed to write something. I remember the agony I would go through when I had to write a paper on some topic in school as an assignment. Thank God my oldest sister, Beverly, would write my essays for me. She was smart, got A's, and read a lot. In the years after I turned 30, my learning disability lessened, but it was still challenging.

I was also dyslexic. Numbers and letters interchanged. So, I had a tough time sounding out words and reading. If someone gives me a phone number or spells their last name, they often need to repeat themselves 3 – 4 times before I can get it correctly. This disability limited my employment opportunities, and I am also still challenged with phonics.

After the sexual abuse, I was put in a special reading group, which was embarrassing and shameful. There were 3 of us singled out in my class. Again, I felt like a dummy; something was wrong with me. Going to Sunday School was agonizing too, as we sometimes took turns reading the Bible. My teacher always had to help me read a few sentences.

My dad was also often inappropriate with women, hugging and touching them where he shouldn't have. In his 70s, my dad printed out "Hug Cards" and received a hug from almost every waitress. This upset all of us daughters and my mother, and we scolded him, but he ignored us. What could my mother have done? She had lots of fears, too. Once, my sister Beverly asked our mom, why don't you get a divorce? My mother replied, "How would I support myself, and where would I live?" My mother thought she had to have a husband to survive, which was probably true then.

Life Learning Point:

As a parent, be extra careful not to leave your children unattended. Most sex offenders are relatives (father, uncle, cousin, etc.), close friends, or neighbors. Teach your children what is appropriate and inappropriate touching and behavior. Teach them to yell "Stop" if something seems wrong. The statistics are staggering on how many children are sexually abused. Here are some books that can help you teach your children to stay safe: https://www.parentsprotect.co.uk/books-to-read-with-children-to-help-prevent-sexual-abuse.htm

***

In grammar school, junior high, and high school, I had one thing that made me feel sort of okay. It was sports, a significant gift since I struggled to function normally. I always did the best in my class for whatever sport we did. I won the tetherball tournament and placed first in a hula hoop contest in grammar school. In Junior high, I did well in GAA sports. In 9th grade, I swam on the high school team, but my skin broke out in red hives from the Chlorine, and I had to quit. That was a gift because the following year, in 10th grade, I went out for the tennis team and made it even though I had never played tennis before. In my senior year, I played number one on the team and was voted most valuable female player. Playing tennis well was valuable as it opened many social and professional doors throughout the rest of my life.

While attending high school, I usually went to the Fresno City Library every night after dinner to study. I went up into the stacks where there were dividers so I could isolate myself. I had a low attention span; I couldn't have any distractions or noise to accomplish even simple assignments. I studied every night in junior high and high school to get "C's." I did this because I wanted to attend college and become a Physical Education teacher. The only thing I knew how to do well was play sports.

At age 15, I started feeling anxious. Perhaps it was because my hormones began to flow, and in my mind, sexual feelings were bad. I didn't know what to do. But I noticed if I emotionally overate, the anxiety would go away. I often binged on cookies, ice cream, and trail mix. I got in the habit of doing my shameful behavior at night when no one was around. This happened 3 – 4 nights a week. I was out of control and felt guilty and ashamed. Over the next 22 years, I was addicted to binge eating to numb my feelings. It was excruciatingly emotionally painful to lose the weight, look great, and regain it all back four months later. This happened four times.

At 16, my oldest sister, Beverly, who was 5 ½ years older, started taking me places with her because she felt sorry for me, and she didn't want me to be left at home alone with our mother. Beverly and her boyfriend Bill took me snow skiing, which was life-saving. She also took me to the coffee shop, where she met friends, and they visited for hours. I enjoyed being with the group even though I hardly spoke. I just sat there and listened, occasionally nodding my head. I had no opinions.

My other sister Shirley, four years older, was busy with her friends. She was quite a social butterfly, and I think a little boy crazy. We didn't have that much interaction that I can remember growing up, as she was always gone with her friends. Shirley got married the week after she graduated from high school.

When I was 19, I tried out and became a volunteer National Ski Patroller for our local ski area. This was just what I needed. I gained some confidence and earned respect from the other Ski Patrol members. Over the next ten years, I volunteered for many positions in our local organization. I taught first aid, trained others to operate a sled, took avalanche training, and taught search and rescue exercises. One year, I was the Mountaineering Director for the Far West Division, and we took a three-day trip on skins (cross-country), sleeping in snow caves we dug. I also became the Patrol Leader of our 130-member club. During this time, I was taking baby steps toward gaining confidence and feeling comfortable socially. At the end of the ten years, I was awarded an International National Ski Patrol #4053 for my service.

For the next 25 years, I volunteered for everything. However, it was not until later in life that I realized I was volunteering to try and feel good about myself and prove my worth. Not having self-worth drove me to volunteer for everything that came before me. Looking back, I was the Director of over 15 major events that involved hundreds of people and took months to organize without earning a penny.

I have always worked. When I was 10, I watered a neighbor's garden and lawn all summer that covered 1½ acres. When I was 12, I also started babysitting. My first job was caring for three children, 5, 3, and 6 months. When I think about it, I can't believe someone would leave a young girl with three children; I was a child myself. I remember staring at the six-month-old baby while he slept in the crib, hoping he wouldn't wake up.

At home, I mowed the large lawn in the front yard and the small backyard. I vacuumed the house, dusted, and occasionally helped Mother with laundry; we had a Maytag wringer washing machine, and I helped her hang the clothes on the line for drying.

While attending high school, I worked at a fast-food restaurant after school and on the weekends.

I paid for all my expenses: clothes, ski and tennis equipment, education, and social activities. My parents did provide me with an older car and paid for the insurance, which I am grateful for.

My brother, Al, six years younger than me, was an unplanned child, but when I told my dad that the new baby was a boy, he was so excited that he ran from the barn where he was milking the cow and straight through a barbed wire fence to get to the house.

My mother felt that a boy would bring her more respect and love from her husband. Al was treated like a golden child. He learned at a young age that his parents would do everything for him.

When he was growing up, Al was not required to mow the lawn or have duties around the home, and he didn't play sports like his older sisters. When he graduated from High School, Al worked for a friend of the family building large wood tanks for the wineries. Then, in his early 20s, he started a company with a friend to build hot tubs. This was short-lived, as he had no experience running a business.

My parents owned a mobile home by the river in Fresno, and Al lived there for several years. Later, I found out that Al lived rent-free. In the meantime, my parents purchased some land at an auction with my dad's aunt. It was over a hundred acres that had redwood trees in the Santa Cruz mountains on the coast of California. After this property was divided with my dad's aunt, my parents ended up with about 35 acres, which was flatter, and my aunt got 100+ hilly acres.

My brother moved to the property and built a small one-room building. He lived there for several years. No responsibilities. No bills. My parents were paying the taxes. However, my brother did get his contractor's license, which was a big deal. A friend of Al's who owned land nearby hired him as the general contractor for building two homes.

Next, my brother wanted to build a home on the property. He asked Mom and Dad for a $60,000 loan. My parents agreed, refinanced their free and clear house, and gave Al the money. The agreement was Al would make the monthly mortgage payments of $611. I believe Al made 2 to 3 payments, and that was it. After that, whenever

I visited my parents in Fresno, they would complain about how tight money was and how they couldn't afford anything. But they did not complain about Al, and they did not insist Al make payments as promised. Perhaps it was because they still owned the land.

My brother lived in a small, lovely mountain home for years without paying taxes or fire insurance. And every time my parents came for a visit, they brought bags of food.

In 1995, our father's health was failing, and my parents deeded the property to my brother, so he owned the home and property without debt. Al was in his early 40s then and had not worked much in the past 20 years.

Then, in February of the following year, my dad called for a family meeting. My two sisters, and brother, and I sat with our parents around the dining room table. My dad announced he was going to sell their investment property, comprised of one house and three apartments, to Al and his friend. Thank God, my sister Beverly jumped up and yelled: "Like hell, you are! That investment property is going to take care of Mother when you are gone!" That was the end of the conversation.

My parent's behavior showed how needy they were of their son's love and approval. There was no good reason to sell their investment property to Al. Al already had a property worth over a million dollars that was given to him. And the investment property was essential to take care of our mother when Dad was gone.

I am deeply grateful to my sister Beverly, who stood up to our dad and Al. I would not have been able to do it myself. If it weren't for Beverly, all the girls would probably experience a hardship caring for our mother. Plus, I would not have received any inheritance from my mother's passing ten years later, which was critical to my healing at that time. Two months later, our dad passed away.

In his mid-40s, Al reconnected with Cindy, a friend he had known for a long time. Cindy had returned to California after working in Washington. Cindy's parents had offered to build her a new home on a 19-acre parcel if she moved back. They missed her. While the home was being built, this is when Cindy and Al got together as a couple. Cindy thought Al was a very responsible man for owning a house on a large property without debt. She had no idea of the truth. When they married, she discovered Al had a deep fear regarding money. This was logical as he was not self-reliant and had earned very little of what he owned.

Our parents had conditioned him to be a complainer and whine about how hard it was to make a living. As a result, Al's life focused on how to get out of work and do as little as possible. This is the conditioning he received growing up.

After getting married, they lived in Al's house in the Santa Cruz mountains. When Cindy's home was finished, they moved into it and rented Al's home. After a short time, they realized they needed a more stable income, so Al sold his home and did a 1031 exchange for some income property in Nevada, a Jiffy Lube, where he received a substantial monthly check without doing much.

I remember visiting Al for the first time in his new home, and Cindy complained that Al would not retrieve phone calls because he refused to learn how to work the answering machine. I told Al, "You have got to learn to get phone messages; it is so easy." Then, I showed him how to push "play" and listen to the messages. Then I explained, "If you want to delete the message, just press delete; otherwise, the message will be saved."

When Al and Cindy had a baby girl, she purchased a cell phone just in case of an emergency in the car with their baby. The cost was $20 per month. Al was so mad that Cindy spent the money, and he didn't talk to her for a week. I told her that was abusive. And at the same time, Al was drinking several beers every night.

Another time I visited, I spent several hours teaching Al to turn on the computer and search the internet using Google. Until then, he had refused to learn how to operate a computer. He expected Cindy to do everything. Our mother had raised Al to depend on others to care for him, and he demanded it.

Cindy was a great cook and a wonderful mother who cared for their daughter as a baby and growing up. Cindy did projects with her daughter, helped with schoolwork, and taught her good values, such as caring for sick and abandoned rescue dogs.

When I visited, Al teased Cindy about needing to get a job so it would pay for the family health insurance. Of course, this upset Cindy because she was doing all the work around the house and raising their daughter while Al wasn't doing much.

But there are always two sides to a story. Cindy was a sweet girl, and when they first got married, I noticed that she waited on Al hand and foot, kept the house clean, and cooked delicious, healthy meals.

Cindy was a kind and generous woman who wasn't into confrontations, which probably meant she sacrificed too much of herself to keep the peace.

What I did was unhealthy, too! I had supported Al emotionally all his life. I used to call his home every month or two to stay connected. When I called the house, and Al was not home, Cindy and I talked, and she would open up and share Al's disrespectful behavior. I tried to share with her that this is just how Al was raised and to accept it. That was my big mistake, which I deeply regret and apologize for. If I were healthier, I would have told Cindy, "You've got to get healthy boundaries." But I didn't. I was conditioned not to see the truth regarding family members and to support them no matter what.

I don't believe Cindy was raised in a household that encouraged her to have healthy boundaries and stand up for herself. She didn't have the opportunity to make mistakes and learn. However, Cindy did ask Al to do something to give back to the community since he was not working, but he refused. After two years, they got a divorce.

I deeply regret not telling Al the truth about his behavior and that he would lose his wife if he didn't start being respectful to her. Unfortunately, I didn't have the insight and strength to share this information with him then, and I sincerely apologize to Al and Cindy.

Unfortunately, this is what happens in a lot of marriages. One person has weak boundaries, and the other keeps doing what they want until the first person can no longer stand it and asks for a divorce. By then, they may be bitter, resentful, and misbehave. But they are finally done being a victim of disrespect!

I have learned that if you have a problem in your relationship, ask yourself what part of the problem you are responsible for. Is it that you don't have healthy boundaries? Are you not contributing enough, being disrespectful, or irresponsible in some areas? Are you not willing to change or get help?

We all make mistakes. If we spend time with a person we just met and there is mutual attraction, we should know both parties are on their best behavior. We should be careful not to ignore red flags and sweep them under the rug. I did that a lot. If you pay attention, people reveal themselves by what they do and say early on.

Life Learning Point:

People reveal who they are early on if you are conscious and aware of what they do and communicate. Be careful not to sweep red flag behavior under the rug.

***

I have suffered from homelessness twice, two years each time. I didn't think, "Poor me," I just kept putting one foot in front of the other because I didn't think I had any other choice. I knew little about how my dad betrayed me, and my mother did not protect me.

When I was homeless, Al never offered me any support of any kind. You might be thinking, why didn't I ask? When I was in Carson City, dog and house sitting, and Al and his daughter visited for a few days, I furnished the meals and was happy to do so. It was great to spend time with his daughter, Vanessa and Al.

About a month later, Al called and said he planned to pick up his daughter again and asked if they could come stay with me again for a few days. I thought that would be nice, and I asked him for $20 for groceries since I was living off my social security check of $800 and money was tight. To my surprise, he got angry, raised his voice, and said: "I've got bills, too, you know!" He was upset and insulted that I asked for grocery money. I thought to myself, wow, thanks to our parents, you get a big check in the mail every month without doing much. I had been conditioned not to see the truth about my family. But at that moment, I could see the truth about Al for the first time. My emotions were mixed with hurt, anger, and sadness. After we got off the phone, I did not hear back from Al.

One of the reasons I am sharing this information about my parents and brother is to illustrate the importance of parents raising self-reliant children. This is the most significant gift a parent can provide. If children do not feel safe and learn to be self-sufficient, they often become anxious when they leave school and home because they have not learned the skills to care for themselves.

Why and how my parents raised my two sisters and me so differently from their only son was unhealthy. All the girls are hard-working and athletic. My brother Al is not. I felt hurt to be treated so differently when I struggled so much.

Children at age 12 can learn to do their laundry, prepare simple meals, and keep their bedrooms picked up and clean. My friend Ginny said she started helping her children pick up their toys and put them in the toybox when they were toddlers. Both of her sons, as adults, are ambitious and had great jobs (they are retired now).

Another friend who is very successful in his career and makes excellent money insisted his children in high school have a job during the weekends and summers. His children learned how to work and be self-reliant, a true gift. Both children are now successful adults supporting themselves.

When I was in junior high school, my oldest sister Beverly started dating a man named Bill. He was an only child and liked to spend time at our house because we always had a lot going on. Bill felt sorry for me and started helping me with my algebra homework. He also said I was not stupid a few times, which surprised me. For the first time, besides my sister Beverly, someone believed in me.

Bill was a nice guy, but he didn't have the incentive to finish college. He was an only child with a new car and credit card. He had a double major and went to class during the day, and at night, he would meet Beverly and friends at the coffee shop and visit for hours. On the other hand, my sister Beverly was ambitious, paying for all her expenses, attending college during the day, and working nights at

Denny's as a waitress. As a result, she often spent a short time socializing at the coffee shop while others spent hours visiting.

After a few years, Beverly broke up with Bill and started dating another man. In the meantime, Bill would come over to the house occasionally, and I would see him at the coffee house gatherings. By this time, I knew all the friends that met nightly. They were nice to me, even if I didn't talk much. During this time, I had no opinions and felt awkward and insecure. I only spoke occasionally, but mostly just sat and listened.

When I was beginning my senior year in high school, Bill and I did an event together that I don't remember, but he showed me he was interested in me as a relationship. It was initially uncomfortable because I always considered Bill as a supportive friend. But for the next five years, we were a couple.

When I graduated from college, I think I lost some respect for him as he was still attending college and had not graduated. I was 22, and Bill was 27 and still not working. Bill broke up with me and started dating a beautiful massage therapist. I was crushed. I must confess I knew nothing about healthy relationships, boundaries, and caring for myself. Bill had taken care of me since I was 17. Now, I was alone and on my own.

Bill ended up marrying a girlfriend of mine, Terry, in the Ski Patrol, which I was delighted about. Becoming a husband and father, Bill changed his ways and became ambitious and a good provider.

When I went to Fresno City College, I studied a lot and worked part-time as a Recreation Leader at a local elementary school after school and on the weekends.

I paid for all my expenses except my parents furnished me with an older car and paid for the insurance. In those days, education was inexpensive.

In 1967, after taking a final examination in summer school at Fresno City College, I drove up to Shaver Lake, which was in the mountains, where my family was gathering on a houseboat. I had not eaten lunch when I arrived around 2 p.m. and was given a strong margarita even though I didn't drink. I was almost 20 years old. What we did that afternoon, I don't remember. I only remember lying on a hard surface in the early evening, in my swimsuit, in the cabin they rented. One of my sisters shouted, "Open the door," and heavy knocking. At that moment of awakening, someone had their finger up my vagina. I was shocked, but I pretended to be asleep. My dad, my brother-in-law-to-be, and a best friend of the family were left with me alone in the cabin while my mother and two sisters had gone for a walk. They had returned early because my mother had turned her ankle.

My brother-in-law-to-be carried me to a small trailer outside the cabin where I slept. The following day, no one asked me anything, no one said anything, and like many sexual abuse cases, it was all swept under the rug as if nothing happened. However, I feel that the women in my family probably suspected something had happened, but I don't remember anyone asking me about it.

Again, this sexual abuse was extremely upsetting. When a father encourages other men to sexually abuse their daughter, this feels like the lowest thing anyone could do. At the time, I was numb, and I pushed down my feelings. I didn't talk to anyone or tell anyone. It wasn't until I took a class 25 years later that I shared the truth for the first time and knew it was not my fault and I wasn't bad. A father is supposed to protect his daughter, not encourage other men to sexually assault her. How can anyone feel good about themselves when their father promotes sexual abuse? This whole incident was confusing and degrading, and I felt like the scum of the earth.

My dad was emotionally unhealthy. On the one hand, he was generous and kind, and on the other hand, he had a dark side and unresolved mental health issues of his own.

I felt terrible about myself, but knowing and acknowledging the truth about my parents was unsafe. I still could not feel anger and continued binge eating to numb myself.

After graduating from Fresno City College, I attended the University of California at Fresno for three years. I wanted to be a Physical Education teacher. I took an extra year to get through college and earned a BA Degree and teaching certificate.

When I graduated from college, I got my first teaching job in Sanger, a small community 20 miles Southeast of Fresno. I also moved into my first apartment. I was so excited. I had worked hard to get through school, and now I would live independently and teach for the first time.

I thought it would be smooth sailing from this moment forward. However, my first year of teaching was disappointing and traumatizing. Not having healthy boundaries, I invited co-workers, students, and others to take advantage of me personally and professionally. At that time, I had no idea what healthy boundaries were. I was immature and emotionally unhealthy.

This caused me tons of emotional pain, resentment, and regret. Not being able to say "no" out of the fear of being rejected also cost me giving in sexually to a few dates, which created a massive amount of guilt and shame.

Life Learning Point:

Healthy boundaries and good emotional health are essential in every area of life if you want to be happy, healthy, and successful!

***

Not having healthy boundaries and having some characteristics of my mother, such as being controlling, were a horrible combination; I failed miserably. The teaching was good, but as a PE teacher in those days, a teacher had to coach a sport. A few athletes challenged me. After the second year, I quit. I was a nervous wreck. I felt very alone with no one to talk to. The other PE teachers were unsupportive, and I felt like an outsider. The disappointment was overwhelming, and again, I numbed myself by binge eating.

The following year, I moved in with Betsy back in Fresno. She was a great roommate. I got a part-time teaching position at McLane High School, except now I had to teach a class in biology, which was my minor. I felt sorry for my students because my lectures were boring. I just followed the manual for the course. Some of the kids were challenging, too.

One day, before class started, the school's principal entered my classroom and sat in the back. I was nervous; however, all the students noticed the guest and sat there like little angels. I was grateful but stressed out. I know now if I were to teach a biology class, I would do things differently and teach students skills that are valuable for everyday living. But, of course, I now have a wealth of information about human behavior and life skills that I didn't have then.

While teaching PE and biology at this new high school, I started taking night classes and received my Master's in Physical Education. I thought the kids were the problem. I didn't have a clue that I was the problem. I thought I could be successful if I taught school at the junior college level.

Wrong. In my 6th year of teaching, I got a job at the University of California, Chico. My responsibilities were coaching volleyball and tennis along with PE classes. I had some experience with both sports but didn't have enough knowledge and experience at the university level, and I failed miserably. I was overly critical of myself, utterly stressed, and massively disappointed again, and I quit. It felt like decades of effort had gone down the drain.

One of my office mates, George, had gotten a divorce a year before. We went out to dinner often because he was lonely, and I knew no one in Chico when I arrived. As with many relationships, we became a couple after being friends and spending several months together. When I decided to quit my job, George invited me to move in with him.

Next, I got my real estate license and worked in that field for four years.

In December of the 3rd year, I volunteered to put on the Board of Realtors and Chico Tennis Club's Christmas Parties. When George and I danced at the Board of Realtors Christmas Party, he looked happy and proud of me, smiling ear to ear; I had just been acknowledged for putting on a great party.

The very next night was the tennis club's Christmas party. A friend, Debbie, with whom I had played tennis, said she wasn't attending because she didn't want to go alone. So, I invited her to sit at our table of 8. Debbie seemed super impressed with George when she discovered he had played for the 49ers. Debbie was 18 years younger than George. Four weeks later, I found out they were having an affair. It was gut-wrenching. I could hardly function. I was shocked, felt betrayed, and deeply hurt. I moved out immediately.

I took a three-day relationship class in San Francisco, took the four-day EST Training in Sacramento, and started going to therapy for the first time. As enthusiastic as I was about the classes and professional help, my feelings about myself didn't change much. I still felt horrible.

The first year after our breakup, I kept bumping into my two exes because Chico was a small town then. That was uncomfortable. And because the home loan interest rates had increased to 18%, selling real estate was undesirable, and I decided it would be a good time to leave town. So, one night, after a recreational basketball game and while all of us girls were having pizza and beer, an acquaintance, Barbara, and I talked about going on a snow ski trip. A week later, Barbara called me and said she was ready to go, and off we went on our adventure.

It was Feb 1982 when we arrived in Aspen. Barbara, who came to Aspen with me, met an Australian the first night we arrived, and after three months, he took her back home, and they married.

I worked at the Aspen Racquet Club and found a lovely home to live in by doing maid work and paying $300. I had a private bedroom downstairs. The landlord, David, who lived in Denver, would come to Aspen on the weekends, always bringing his buddies to hunt and fish. After they left, I would change all the bedsheets and clean the house. It was a great home overlooking Aspen. I liked David; he was easy to get along with, and I was allowed to have gatherings at the house.

I worked at the Aspen Racquet Club, which was terrific. I got to know a lot of people. My manager, Candy, was great; we had many tennis events for the members. At that time, the Aspen Racquet Club was a bubble with three tennis courts inside and eight courts outside in the summer. We worked in a shack literally; I answered the phone, took reservations, paired people to play in tournaments, and helped with the billing.

While working at the tennis club, I met my now husband, Kenny. At that time, Kenny was happily married with three children. Always being early, Kenny would come to the club, and we would chat and joke before he played his matches. Sometimes, we would play mixed doubles together in tournaments. We were good friends.

Aspen was so much fun and so beautiful! There was always something going on: a World Cup Race, state and national competitions in rugby, volleyball, and ice hockey, lots of music at the Tent each week, places to go dancing, and weekly concerts on the Hill at Snowmass. My friend Ginny and I hiked from Aspen to Crested Butte with a group. This is what locals often do annually. We had picnics in the park, hikes with blooming flowers, bike rides, skiing, celebrity tennis tournaments, and concerts - the most memorable was Dionne Warwick's. I also played on the lady's "Wild Flower's softball and soccer team." I also met Candace White, a social butterfly who introduced me to lots of people and always included me in fun events. I felt like a local since I knew many people from my club. When I walked around Aspen, I always knew many people to say hello to and have coffee with. It was fun and games for three and a half years, even though I was still binge eating to numb myself.

Living in Aspen was a special time, except I thought I should be doing something more with my life professionally and earning more money. Since I had put on many large, successful tennis tournaments over the past ten years, I started researching and applying for jobs with sports marketing companies. Finally, I connected with Gary in Santa Barbara, who said he needed someone to organize celebrity tennis tournaments in that area. We talked over the phone, and I left for California. My new friend Candace White also moved to Santa Barbara while returning to where she had raised her children.

Remember my three-year-old traumatic incident when I made up the belief it wasn't safe to ask questions? I was mortified to ask questions, afraid they might get angry, which meant I would be unsafe. When I got to Santa Barbara, Gary said he could not pay me then, but after the two tournaments were complete in 5 months, he would pay me $10,000. I knew that was not a good idea, but I was still trying to prove my worth, and now I had nothing else going on in this new location. I signed a contract. I know you are thinking, "What a stupid girl. You never sign an agreement to do work before you get at least half of the payment upfront." Yes, I was foolish, gullible, and unprofessional.

I spent the next five months recruiting players to partner with the celebrities already lined up and handling many other details. The first tournament was in Santa Maria, 76 miles north of Santa Barbara. It took a lot of effort to talk 16 people into paying to play with a celebrity. I also recruited a few friends to organize a gourmet luncheon for 60 people. The Mary Hart & Jimmy Messina Celebrity Tennis Tournament in Santa Barbara also went very well. At the end of 5 months, Gary said the tournaments didn't earn enough to pay me. I was upset because I had been meagerly living off my credit cards, staying with friends, dog, and house-sitting. Again, I was a victim, and it was all my fault. I didn't know how to take care of myself. If I did a great job, I thought people would be fair with me and keep their agreements. Wrong! What I did was certainly not a good business practice.

When a person has sabotaging beliefs, they constantly behave from these limiting beliefs. In my case, I was operating from the beliefs that I created as a three-year-old. They ran my life and caused me great disappointment, resentment, and struggle.

The following year, Gary bad-mouthed me to the tennis club manager, who knew what a great job I had done. I took Gary to the Employment Court and won the case. The Judge even awarded me two thousand dollars extra because my payment was delayed. I was pleased, but immediately, Gary filed for bankruptcy and moved out of California. Again, this was another big disappointment and further supported my belief that people betray me. My limiting beliefs were causing emotional pain and hardship over and over again. Some say that the Universe keeps giving you the lesson until you learn. I am not sure if that is correct. It is more like you keep attracting the same circumstances until you clear the sabotaging beliefs causing the problem.

Life Learning Point:

Even though a person seems friendly and honest, some people will lie and take advantage of others if they feel their livelihood is threatened. I have experienced this several times in my life. It's better to get an agreement in writing with specific details to make people accountable for their promises.

***

Next, I was asked to be the Volunteer Director for the First Santa Barbara Film Festival. I organized over 180 volunteers for the three-day event, from selling tickets at an office downtown to assigning drivers to the celebrities and ushers for each film. This volunteer job was more than full-time for two months. I only went to the closing film because they wanted to acknowledge me.

I lived in Santa Barbara for another 21 years but never attended another Santa Barbara Film Festival because I could not afford the tickets. When I think back on this whole situation, I think how foolish I was to spend two months working seven days a week to make the first Santa Barbara Film Festival a huge success without asking for anything in return. If I had been emotionally healthy and felt good about myself, I could have requested two-lifetime passes, which they would gladly have given me. Instead, I experienced another major disappointment and heartbreak.

Again, my victim behavior reflected my 3-year-old trauma when I created the limiting belief, "It is not safe for me to ask for anything."

Next, my friend Candace White from Aspen asked me if I wanted to take a class at Unity Church with her.

The course was "Lighten Up," given by one of the church members, a therapist named Jan Clinton.

This class was life-changing. It was all about feeling your emotions and expressing them. The course was weekly, and on the third meeting, Jan said we would get in touch with our anger by hitting rubber mallets on large stuffed pillows. When Jan made the rounds and came to our twosome, she asked, "Why aren't you hitting your pillow?" I said, "Because I am not angry about anything, and I don't have any anger." That was a foolish and untrue statement. I had spent 36 years numbed out and inauthentic, and I didn't even know it. And I had used my binging eating addiction to go numb.

I had no idea that having all types of emotions was healthy and that it was good to feel them. I had been conditioned to think just the opposite. I remember Jan being forceful and saying, "Start hitting, for practice's sake." Reluctantly, I started hitting the pillow, and after 5-6 minutes, some anger did come up. Then, after another

5 minutes, I felt my rage, which I had not experienced since my three-year-old tantrum. I was using the rubber mallet like I was trying to kill someone. I had allowed my stuffed-down rage to surface, and I was acting like a crazy person hitting the pillow. When I was through, I was sweating and exhausted, and I had a blister on one of my fingers. I felt a massive release that had been stuffed down for over 36 years out of fear of being punished.

Every week, our assignment was to meet with a partner outside class and practice expressing our emotions. When we felt fear, we would stand and shake. And when we felt anger, we would use a rubber mallet. The class was 12 weeks long, which I took three times over 14 months. And like magic, at the end of the 3rd class, **I did not have a binge eating disorder and lost 20 pounds**. This was a miracle. I had been trying desperately to lose weight and keep it off for over two decades without success. I then decided to commit to doing whatever it took to feel good about myself.

From that time on, every birthday until I was 70 years old, I wished to become emotionally healthy before I blew out the candles on my cake. So that was my journey for the next 30 years. Taking classes and learning coaching and healing modalities were my number one priority.

A year later, I learned about a class provided by a nonprofit for those sexually abused. We first met in a large room where about 70 people gathered. We had a speaker who gave a short talk; then, we broke into small groups of about 8 – 10 women. Everyone shared their story of being sexually abused. It was the first time I had ever talked to anyone about mine. In this class, I learned it wasn't my fault and that I was not bad.

When others shared their stories, I wanted to weep. Professionals who lead the class explained that 37% of women experience sexual abuse. To me, this sounded like an unbelievably huge percentage. We were also told that most of the sexual abuse perpetrators are a relative (uncle, cousin, father, etc.) or good friends of the family. In my experience of coaching others with sexual abuse, I have always found this to be true. When I completed this three-month class, I felt relieved, and another huge weight lifted off my shoulders. Today, the percentages are slightly better; 25% of all women experience sexual abuse, which still seems alarming to me. Men also get abused as children, but at a lesser percentage.

The following professional step I took was helping nonprofits with their events. One fundraising event, Day on Centre Court, was on 16 private tennis courts where I assigned five teams in which they did a round-robin tournament. Gourmet lunches were delivered to the private home courts, and then all the winners of each court played in the finals at the park the next day. The next evening, we also had a silent auction, dinner, band, and dancing at a private estate in Montecito. Again, the event was very successful.

I also put on the USTA National Tennis Hardcourt Championships for men 70, 75, 80, 85 & 90 for three consecutive years. We had nametags, a program with all the players' names, addresses, and phone numbers, a welcome luncheon, trophies, and a dinner banquet at a nice hotel. Now that I have played in ten National Tournaments myself over the past four years, I know what we did for the players was way beyond what other tournaments do.

These events were fun for me to do and organize; I was good at it. But because I had low self-esteem, my hourly wage turned out to be low, which was almost impossible to live on in Santa Barbara.

My next job in 1990 was working for the Santa Barbara City College Foundation. They hired me partly to help organize fundraising and donor cultivation events for the President of the College. My Executive Director, Jim, also gave me the job of overseeing the Scholarship Program. I created an excellent program with all the donors' names and scholarship recipients. In addition, I initiated a program where the scholarship recipients wrote a letter to the donor thanking them for the scholarship and what it meant to them to receive it. I loved this job because I felt I was helping many students and their future.

But again, not having healthy boundaries, I took on too many responsibilities and found myself working until 7 or 8 p.m. and coming in on Saturdays. Finally, after five years, I was burnt out, stressed, and quit.

Life Learning Point:

Self-esteem doesn't come from doing; it just is. Many people have been conditioned to be doers, always having to accomplish tasks and goals to feel okay about themselves and please others. This comes from childhood trying to please their parents to meet their needs. Or if their parents are big doers, children often get their parent's habits and conditioning. The truth is a person has value and worth without doing anything.

***

One personal development course I took was four days in Los Angeles, called Warrior. On Saturday, the third day, the leader casually mentioned that some volunteers were preparing the coals for a fire walk that evening. I immediately thought, "No way, I would never do that in a million years."

That evening, after the leader had gone over the rules and had us sign a disclaimer, he told us that if we didn't get a "yes" after we asked," Should I walk?" under no circumstances should we participate. We started chanting a short phrase that I thought I'd never forget, but I did. After 10-15 minutes, someone stepped up and walked across the 10-foot lane of coals. I was mesmerized. Then, several other people walked across. After an hour of watching people repeatably walking over the coals, the leader announced that it was the last call for anyone who hadn't gone.

I decided to stand by the end of the line where people walked over the coals. The leader reminded us if you don't get a firm "yes" to walk, don't go. As I stood there with my arms by my side, my fingers became deformed, and I went into an altered state. And without warning or asking, I walked over the coals. At the end of the coals, I fell into a burly man's arms, sobbing. He held me tight and sprayed water on my feet. I was safe. I guess the lesson here is not to say “never.”

As I mentioned earlier, I had committed to improving myself. So, from 1989 – 1997, I got involved with Landmark Education and took all their classes and seminars except one. These classes took dozens of trips to the Los Angeles area from Santa Barbara, a three-and-a-half-hour trip each way. I have listed all of them at the end of the book with the massive number of other classes and training I have taken.

In the year-long Wisdom Course, part of Landmark Education, we had weekly meetings they called parties, plus three-weekend classes in the Los Angeles area. We made a binder, two pages representing every year of our life. Those two pages contained a picture of those in our close community. We made a list of anything that happened that was upsetting and the limiting beliefs we created. In addition, we collaged the major sabotaging beliefs we had. This was helpful. I had over 30 significant collages. When the class ended, out of the 30 limiting beliefs, only about half were gone. Even though I knew who, how, when, and where I got the limiting belief, some were still operating.

The following year, I volunteered to coach the local participants in hopes of removing my remaining limiting beliefs. But this did not happen. **Beliefs like "Men leave me" and "I am powerless" remained.**

Life Learning Point:

Just because you know the limiting beliefs operating, how you got them, when, where, and why, other associated limiting beliefs may need to be cleared first before the original belief can be removed.

***

In 1993, I participated in my first Sprint Triathlon, a quarter-mile swim in the ocean, a six-mile bike ride, and a two-mile run. In the five years I raced, I won first place in my age group, 45- 49, four times. I could hardly believe all my times were under 60 minutes, and I am proud of this accomplishment since I was not a runner.

In 1995, I started life coaching with a few clients. I always had various jobs that paid the bills while working with one or two clients. It was challenging, but I was driven to get emotionally healthy, feel good about myself, and care for myself financially, which was always a big fear.

In 1996, four months before I turned fifty, one of my girlfriends, Arianna, asked me what I wanted to do to celebrate. I knew someone who had hiked Mount Whitney, so I suggested that. Arianna, another friend, Miriam, and I started training for the 22-mile round-trip hike. One week before my 50th birthday, September 25th, we hiked the highest peak in the Intercontinental US, 14,498 feet elevation. It took us 20 hours. I think we broke the record for taking the longest time, but it was a magical and spiritual trip. Great weather, not a leaf blowing, and a gorgeous full moon. We were blessed. The following weekend, it stormed, which would have prevented us from making the hike.

In 1998, I enrolled in Coach University, a 2-year online course founded by the late Thomas Leonard. It is a great school. In the second year, they offered an Introduction to the Emotional Freedom Technique (EFT), which some people know as tapping. I was enthused as I needed something more substantial to clear my limiting beliefs. I took the basic and advanced EFT training in Los Angeles and started using the healing method to remove phobias and other emotions in myself and others.

After taking these classes, I also worked with a therapist who had taken the EFT classes, and we traded weekly sessions for one year.

Regarding relationships, when I lived in Santa Barbara for 22 years, I had several boyfriends consistently for two years or less. When I was on my own, without a boyfriend, I was okay and felt good about being independent. But when I got into a relationship, I would get needy and insecure, and they would eventually drop me. I experienced emotional pain in my gut whenever they broke up with me, often lasting for months.

Life Learning Point:

The world is a reflection of what is going on inside of us. If you respect yourself, you will attract other people who will respect you. If you feel unworthy, you could attract people who take advantage of you. The lesson is: Look at what you have and see how it reflects your belief system about yourself and life.

***

From 2000 – 2010, I continued to take classes and learn healing modalities. I took the Yuen Method, and again, after completing the training, I traded sessions for one year with a fellow student. I also went to follow-up classes given by a Yuen Healing Practitioner. With the Yuen Method, I learned beliefs are "on" or "off." Meaning a limiting belief can be "on" or "off," and empowering beliefs can be "on" or "off." The goal of healing is to turn "off" the limiting beliefs and turn "on" the empowering beliefs. It is elementary yet complex at the same time.

In 2004, I purchased a Wavemaker for $5,000 and enrolled in a six-month training program for $1200. Tom Stone had gone to Germany to have engineers develop an energy-canceling device. The basics were to find the energy of an unwanted emotion in your body and focus on it while holding probs in both hands that would cancel out the negative energy.

One Friday, when I was driving down to San Diego from Santa Barbara for a class, my car heated up, and I took the first exit off the freeway and went into a gas station. They checked out my car and told me it would be Monday before they could fix a leaky hose. I was upset because I had already paid for my class. I told the mechanic my sad story, and he said, “Wow, you are a lucky girl. There is a train station just a block away.” I walked down the street, waited briefly, and caught a train to San Diego. The Universe had taken care of me again. I was blessed.

I also took a year-long program from Tom Stone to learn about "The 12 Causes of Human Problems” and other valuable information regarding human behavior. Unfortunately, I was one of two of the 18 students from all over the country who did not pass the class. We had to identify a client’s problem within 20 minutes of talking to the client and clear it. I failed.

The following year, I retook the class. However, it was very disappointing because this time, I was the only student in the class that didn't pass. The instructor said I didn't seem intuitive enough, which was true.

I don't know what kept me going. I wanted to quit coaching at least a dozen times, but something inside of me was driving me to hang in there even though, at times, it was highly disappointing. Also, it didn't seem like I would ever be intuitive and be able to help my clients in a big way.

It's even a miracle that I could write this book since I am not a writer. But I wanted to share with people that they can have a happy, healthy, and successful life through my revolutionary success system. I also wanted to let healers, coaches, and wellness professionals know they could enroll in a transformation-proven success system online training so they could be leaders in the field of emotional healing. I have failed a million times, but I am a committed person with unshakable tenacity, which has proved successful beyond what I thought was possible in emotional health and wellness.

> *There are many characteristics that people often attribute to success, but none is more necessary than* ***tenacity****. Without determination and the ability to commit to the task with hard work when passion is quiet, most brilliant ideas would lay dormant and forgotten.* – Mind Fuel Daily

After quitting the Foundation for Santa Barbara City College, I did home care for a famous 88-year-old artist who had lost his short-term memory. I worked 40 hours a week, fixed healthy meals, kept him company, helped him with his artwork as an assistant, and listened to his stories about his life that were interesting (but not so much after hearing them thirty times). He had a routine of swimming laps in his pool, eating breakfast, and then going to his art room. I worked for him for a year. I took on other home care positions for another year to pay the bills.

In 2004, I moved to an apartment that was a converted garage with one bedroom and a kitchenette. I was very excited because, up until that point, I had been living in an apartment with a roommate. This was an opportunity to have a nice place to live and work with clients. Before I moved in, the son of the woman who owned the home said they were renting the garage apartment to keep an eye on their mother, who had a slight loss of memory. He also shared that he needed a garage sale to clear the space. I volunteered to have the garage sale because I wanted to move into the home as soon as possible. I worked organizing all the contents of the apartment they wanted to sell and spent the weekend having a garage sale.

It took me about a month to get everything organized and lovely, with a divider between my office and the living room. I had a beautiful table where my clients could sit, and I could have sessions. There was an outside sliding door where clients could come and go. I was happy. After a few months, it became apparent that the woman's memory was getting worse fast, and her son knew it. He asked me to care for his mother by checking on her morning and night, taking her to beauty parlor appointments, and grocery shopping. In exchange, he would waive my rent, which he did.

This went well until September, nine months after I moved in when the landlady got in a car accident. She was sitting in the back seat without her seat belt, and the person driving hit another car. My landlady hit her head and went to the hospital. After three days, her son informed me that his mother would not be coming home but would go to a senior assisted living community. I asked if I could stay in the house if I found someone to rent the main house, and he said, "Yes."

I placed ads and interviewed several couples. I introduced three couples to the son over the next month. Unfortunately, all of them were unacceptable to him for one reason or another, even though one couple was willing to pay one year's rent in advance.

Then, one day late in November 2004, I got a letter with a thirty-day eviction notice. I was shocked! I had spent time and money on my new home; now it was charming. I had done the yard sale without getting paid, cared for his mother when her short-term memory was gone, and interviewed potential renters. Now, I received a notice without warning. I remember standing there stunned. Then, under my breath, I said something that is, to this day, tough to say because it is so toxic. I said, "This is the beginning of the end."

The next day, I made some phone calls and found another place to move that would have been very nice but expensive. However, I didn't know how I would pay for it, but I didn't think I had any other options. Two weeks later, when packing, I noticed I was uncomfortable getting out of the chair. And then, a few days later, my thighs hurt. In another few days, it was difficult to move without pain. I had no idea what was happening, and I was scared!

I called the landlord of my potentially new home and told her I could not take the cottage in the back of her home. My friend Candace White told me I could stay with her until I figured out what was going on with me physically. I went to my doctor, who gave me some tests, one for inflammation, which was off the charts. He also prescribed female hormones, which did not give me any relief. He didn't know what was causing my pain. After another month of suffering, unable to walk freely, and out of money, I went to the Santa Barbara County Health Department to see if they could help me.

I remember seeing a young doctor doing her internship, and after fifteen minutes of asking me questions, she blurted out, "You have Polymyalgia Rheumatica." I said, "What's that?" She then explained it was an autoimmune disorder where the body attacks itself. Then she said she wanted me to have my lungs x-rayed and that 10% of patients with my condition go blind. She gave me 80 mg of Prednisone. In 50 minutes, the pain in my thighs and shoulders was almost gone, and I could walk again without limping.

Gradually, over the next six weeks, I took less and less Prednisone until I got down to taking 10 mg a day. I was relieved but also worried about the diagnoses my doctor had shared with me. Fortunately, my lungs were okay, and I did not go blind.

Life Learning Point:

When you experience a traumatic situation, be careful what you think and say to yourself or others. During this time, if you say something negative, it can go into your subconscious and manifest. I have heard other tragic stories that support this.

***

Out of money, with my credit cards up to the limits, I filed for bankruptcy because I didn't see any other option. I felt guilty and ashamed. I had always been responsible and kept my agreements, so I felt horrible.

For the next two years, I house-sat, dog, and cat-sat and even took care of a friend's horse, all for free. In those early days, dog and house sitting was new, and most people weren't getting paid. And since I was homeless but not living under the bridge, I didn't think I was in a position to ask for money; I needed a place to sleep. I felt I had to take what I could get. When I didn't have a home to go to, I went to my sister Beverly and her husband John's house in Houston twice, once for seven weeks and once for four weeks. My friend Candace also opened her home to me whenever I needed it, which was a huge blessing and acted as a safety net. I often needed a place to stay between house-sitting for a day or week.

Candace also had many friends who traveled and needed someone to care for their animals. She referred me to lots of house- and dog-sitting jobs.

The Universe provided for me. When one house- and dog-sitting position was up, often another would appear. I remember once the homeowners planned to return by

4 p.m. on a Friday. At noon that day, I got a call from a friend with whom I had a dog- and house-sat before asking if I was available because she had just made reservations to go to Ireland for two weeks. I had another place to live for two weeks. Sometimes, I got to know the owners of the home and their animals, and they were very generous, offering their home for an extra week even though they had returned. I found most people were supportive, but a few were difficult.

In one position, I cared for two horses, a large garden, and watered a yard. The horses took the most time because I had to shovel manure daily from the stalls. And because I was conscientious and took extra care of the 21-year-old cat that was supposed to die, it got better. I stayed there for three months one summer.

In 2005, the first year I was sick with Polymyalgia Rheumatica, I met Faustina Washburn for tea, a friend of mine from college. She was driving an 18-wheeler through Santa Barbara for her job. I so admired her. I told her my story of what had happened to me, having pain and taking Prednisone. She must have known I was struggling financially, too. After our chat, she pulled out her wallet and gave me a stack of twenty-dollar bills that came to three hundred dollars. At that time, I had $34 to my name; that was it. I had to buy a hormone prescription that week, which was $90, and I had other bills due. Receiving this financial support was a surprise and a huge blessing.

Over the next two years, she passed through Santa Barbara three more times. Each time, we met for a brief visit. And again, she pulled out a stack of twenties amounting to three hundred dollars. I will never forget Faustina's kindness and generosity. She was an angel.

You might be asking yourself, why didn't I ask family members for financial help? I think the reason was whenever I talked to anyone, I always said I was okay or good. I was conditioned never to complain or ask for anything at a young age. I know my sisters would have pitched in financially if I had asked.

One year after Dad's death, Mom needed more care. She stayed with an aunt for 3 or 4 months, and then Beverly, my older sister, picked Mom up and took her home to Houston. Our mother needed more care in eight months, and Beverly found a lovely senior assisted living complex. Then, after a year, mother got worse, and Beverly moved Mom to another home. Beverly visited Mom every week for the next eight and a half years before she passed. This was a big commitment that I am deeply grateful for, as the trip to where Mom lived was always about a 50-minute drive each way. Visiting and checking on Mom took almost a whole day of Beverly's life each week. Beverly took her to the hairdressers, out to lunch, to the movies, etc., until it got to the point where Mom had to be in a wheelchair, and she hardly knew her daughter.

In June 2006, my mother passed away. My sister in Fresno sold our mother's income property. In January, my old Ford Tempo broke down at a gas station. I was in the process of selling it, but a mechanic friend came out and looked at the car and suggested that I just give it to the interested buyer because the car wouldn't even start. If I had my car towed away, it would cost money. I called the prospective buyer and told him the situation. He said his cousin lived across the street from the gas station, and he would be over in thirty minutes with friends who could push the car across the street. And that is what happened. Again, the Universe was taking care of me.

This all happened when I was house- and dog-sitting for a lovely couple. I called them when they were out of town and asked if I could use their car if needed, and they said yes. Three days later, I got a check in the mail for my part of my mother's inheritance. Through my Costco membership, I arranged to meet someone at the Honda Dealership in Ventura, thirty miles away. When I arrived, I drove a Honda Civic, which I liked. It was $18,000. However, the salesperson told me they were having a sale that weekend, and I could have a Honda Accord for the same amount.

Wow, the Universe had timed it perfectly. One day, my car broke down, and three days later, I got a check in the mail to buy a new car.

Life Learning Point:

The Universe is always taking care of us, whether we are conscious of it or not. Be thankful!

***

When I lived in Santa Barbara for 22 years, I lived in 14 locations and had nine roommates. During the two years when I was sick and without a home; I estimate I moved 20 times, sometimes every week. It was challenging. Between moves, my car was filled with two suitcases of clothes, my computer, a printer, and four boxes filled with books, client files, and class information from current and past courses. Everything in my car was unpacked and packed every time I moved.

Two years had gone by since I got ill. In January of 2007, I received my inheritance and moved to Austin, Texas, to be closer to my sister, Beverly, and her husband, who lived in Houston. I loved Santa Barbara, but in 22 years, it had been challenging to find affordable housing. Before getting sick, I walked on the beach at least four times per week and hiked the trails regularly. I have tons of great memories of all the beautiful things I did and the people I met. Yes, I struggled, but I also had wonderful experiences and adventures with good friends, and the weather was usually great!

From 2007 through 2009, I spent over $30,000 going to numerous health practitioners and Western medical doctors. I also worked with coaches and healers. Two of the healers used a computer to indicate my body's deficiencies. I did foot baths, and one practitioner regularly put my blood under a microscope and prescribed high-potency vitamins.

Among the many health practitioners that I saw was a pharmacist named Jim. He did some tests on me and said I had seven different parasites in my system. He asked me if I had left the country, and I said, "No." Then, over the next three months, he prescribed products to eliminate my parasites. I am deeply grateful to Jim, as none of the medical doctors or health practitioners had checked for parasites.

Life Learning Point:

When you are emotionally healthy, your immune system is more likely to be strong and fight off parasites and harmful viruses, bacteria, and cancer cells. That is one of the significant reasons why it is critical to have good emotional health.

***

Every doctor and healer I saw got upset when they heard I had been taking 8 – 10 mg of Prednisone daily for years. They said, you have got to get off that stuff; it's damaging to your organs if you take it for an extended time.

I went to a naturopath doctor and a chiropractor, had sessions with healers, did affirmations, and made vision boards. Unfortunately, my health did not improve, but I am grateful to all the health practitioners for keeping me alive.

I traveled to Canada and took a healing class called Matrix Energetics. When I got back, I went to weekly practice meetings.

I traded healing services with a good friend, Aimee, in Austin. I was doing WaveMaker Coaching then, and she was doing ThetaHealing®. I liked what she was doing, so I took the Basic and Advanced classes. Then, for the next year, I traded weekly sessions over the phone with another girl in the class who also had health challenges. In 15 months, after clearing tens of dozens of sabotaging beliefs and emotions, I was off Prednisone, which I had been taking for five years, and was finally pain-free. Healing my emotions and upgrading my "belief system" allowed my body to heal itself. Now, I was profoundly grateful and happy.

This experience further demonstrated to me firsthand the power of the mind-body connection. My body healed when sabotaging beliefs, habits, conditioning, and emotions were cleared. This precious knowledge demonstrated why healthy emotions are critical to physical health. Until I cleared my identity of being a victim, took responsibility for my behavior and results, and removed all of the sabotaging beliefs I created from my childhood trauma, there was no way my body could heal.

Louise Hay wrote a small book outlining physical challenges and their association with limiting beliefs. I now use Dr. Michael Lincoln's book **Messages from the Body**. It is over 700 pages, associating physical challenges with sabotaging beliefs and emotions. Most emotional problems are due to dysfunctional family upbringing, childhood, and adult trauma and abuse, from genes passed down, or from past life experiences.

Once, a client came to our session with a rash on her right forearm. We referred to the book "Messages from the Body." Under Right Forearm. It said: *"How do I get it right?" They are experiencing conflicts and difficulty meeting their needs, wants, and desires and bringing things to the fore. They fear being punished for being inferior or insufficient." Page 61*

My client started laughing and said she had just spent four stressful days at her parent's home for Thanksgiving, which explained everything. She said, "Growing up, I always felt I wasn't good enough."

Another example of the mind-body connection was when I called a girlfriend to see how she was doing. She said she was on the third round of antibiotics to try and heal a bladder infection, but nothing worked. I asked, "Have you been through anything upsetting over the past 4 – 5 months?" She said, "Yes! It took three months to close after submitting an offer to buy a home. The process was very upsetting, and I am angry at the loan officer who let things fall through the cracks."

So, we cleared all her anger, frustration, and exhaustion about buying her home. The session took about an hour and a half. Afterward, she felt much better. We cleared a little more the next day, and she said she felt good. Three days later, her bladder infection was gone.

Life Learning Point:

The body-mind connection is real and powerful. If you have a physical problem or are a practitioner and your client does, it would be wise to consult the "Messages from the Body" or some other reference book to identify and clear the sabotaging beliefs and emotions operating.

***

One of the techniques that I teach all my clients and students is the Core Technique. It is a simple but powerful way to process unwanted emotions. One example of using the Core Technique was a man who had severe stomach problems for seven years. I asked him what had happened just before he started having stomach problems. He thought and thought and finally said, "I had a car accident." I asked him what had happened. He said: "I was driving in a parking lot and hit a pedestrian, and I thought I killed him, but I didn't." We did the CORE technique until the energy in his gut was gone. Afterward, his stomach problem disappeared. You can learn this simple but powerful technique by visiting my website and signing up to receive my free Special Report.

Another example is when I was taking a marketing class in Los Angeles and met a man from Norway during a break. He said he was writing a book about trauma and how it can never be healed. I asked him why he thought that. He said: “Six years ago, my wife was giving a seminar in a third-world country and went to the farmer's market. In the middle of the day, she was stabbed to death." He shared he had tried everything to get over his shock and grief of his wife's death but couldn't. I asked him if he would like to do something that might give him some relief. He said, "Yes." I led him through the CORE Technique for about 25 minutes, and when finished, he said, "Wow, the pain in my gut is gone for the first time since my wife's passing. This is amazing!"

Life Learning Point

Being in touch with your emotions, especially anger, grief, and fear, is critical. Next, you must learn how to process these emotions. (The CORE Technique described in my free Special Report located on my website will help you do this.) Thirdly, any sabotaging beliefs associated with the emotions must be identified and cleared. Fourthly, you must forgive those who hurt or betrayed you and also forgive yourself for your part. If there is no forgiveness, the emotions will only hurt you. Fifthly, you must have healthy boundaries. When you forgive someone, that does not mean you have to spend time with that person, or you may choose to spend a limited amount of time. Warning: if you don't feel and process your traumatic emotions and they get buried alive, they could cause emotional reactions, health problems, or addictions.

***

Using ThetaHealing® and other techniques, I produced better and faster results with my clients. So, I took more ThetaHealing® classes in Idaho and Montana to expand my skill set. I also took the ThetaHealing® Instructor's courses to teach others this powerful healing technique. In the next five years, I taught about 60 students, and some went on and became instructors.

To market my coaching and healing services, I gave dozens of "Introductions" to my healing work and classes at the Austin Unity Church, as well as meet-ups and spiritual groups. As a result, I had a full practice of clients, but I was working 50 hours a week. This continued for about three years.

Then, I stopped giving presentations because they were no longer effective. Lots of people knew about ThetaHealing® by then. Plus, a few new instructors had moved into Austin. After three months, my clients had finished their program, and I only had one new client. I decided to do an experimental group healing class with some volunteers. I was curious how effective this could be. The class worked well, but something kept me from marketing them. I think I feared I wouldn't have enough time because my savings account of $14,000 was draining fast. Also, I started getting stressed about my fear of being unable to pay my bills in another month or two.

I contacted my sister, Beverly, and shared my dilemma. She suggested I come and live temporarily with her and her husband, John, as they wanted to travel. And that is what I did. My emotions were mixed. On the one hand, it was a financial relief; on the other hand, it was extremely disappointing. I was well well-established in Austin's spiritual community with many great friends. Moving to Houston was agonizing. I had come so far, and I loved my beautifully furnished apartment. Now, it felt like I was moving backward, which was true, and again, I failed at taking care of myself.

My sister had a large five-bedroom home. I used one bedroom for my office; another served as my bedroom. My sister and her husband took numerous trips and a cruise while I cared for their dog, cat, one-acre yard, and pool.

After a year, it was time to go, and I started dog- and house-sitting again as I had done eleven years earlier.

One dog- and house-sitting position was in Carson City for three months. The wife I communicated with said she had two dogs, one a poodle that was mainly blind and deaf. I asked her about the challenges of caring for a dog like that, and she said, "Minimal because the dog sleeps most of the time."

The poodle was lovely, but he needed to be by my side continuously. If he weren't, he would bark constantly. He didn't know how to be led with a leash, so I taught him. I took both dogs out twice a day in the large backyard, and they ran around for 30 – 40 minutes. I spent a lot of time teaching the semi-blind dog the perimeters of the yard so he could run around, too. I cooked eggs for the poodle during the first week because he wouldn't eat his regular food. When I care for other people's animals and homes, I think I am more conscientious than the owners.

After six weeks, my ears began to ring. I went to a specialist and got a brain scan. No tumors, gratefully, but it was annoying. I told the owner on our weekly call that the poodle barked non-stop unless I was close by. She seemed upset because I called her out for not disclosing this information.

After this dog-sitting assignment, I drove to my nephew Chris's home between Sacramento and San Francisco, which I used as a home base. The next day, I went to

Berkeley and cared for a dog for Christmas week. On Christmas Eve, I went to an Asian restaurant. I felt comfortable, but I think others around me felt sorry for an old lady sitting by herself.

Then I returned to Chris's home. On the third day, I drove to Oakland and took a plane to Maui, where I cared for two sweet dogs. I had cared for Yvonne's dogs a year before and enjoyed her home, a short block from the beach. That was the best dog- and house-sitting job I ever had. Very relaxing, quiet, and enjoyable. One morning, I woke up and noticed the ringing in my ears was gone. I was profoundly grateful and knew it was more evidence of the mind-body connection.

I joined a hiking and social meet-up group. I had plenty to do. I worked with one client over the phone. I was also taking a Facebook Ad Online Course, which was too difficult to learn. Sometimes, you just need to hire a professional regarding computer stuff when you are in your late 60s and have a learning disability.

The challenges I have shared with you are the tip of the iceberg. I experienced dozens of incidents not mentioned in this book where I allowed marketers and salespeople to take advantage of me because I didn't ask questions. It's difficult for me to admit that I was that emotionally unhealthy.

One of my unusual situations about 20 years ago was when I got an email saying their online program would help me create a website that a monkey could do. That should have been my first clue. After struggling for three days without success, I hired an IT person to help me. After an hour, he said, "I guess I am not as smart as a monkey." We laughed quite a bit before he left my house. That was $600 down the drain, and I felt gullible.

When I returned to California, I spent a week visiting Candace, my elementary school friend, who lived near Napa. We have stayed connected all these years.

Then, I drove to Fresno, where I was born and raised, and visited friends for five days. Next, I drove to Santa Barbara and visited friends for a week. I was filling in time between dog- and house-sitting jobs and making the most of it, enjoying time with good old friends.

Then I drove to Laguna Beach to visit my good friend Ginny, who lives in Basalt, Colorado, but goes to the beach during winter. Ginny told me that our mutual friend from Aspen, Kenny, had lost his wife suddenly.

I mentioned that Kenny was a close friend when I lived in Aspen over thirty years ago. He came to the tennis club where I worked almost daily, and we always had a short visit before he got on the court. We had stayed in touch over the past 30+ years. We met for lunch when Kenny and his wife Carolyn traveled to Santa Barbara. And when I returned to Aspen over the years, I visited them.

Then Ginny said, "Let's call Gracie and wish her a happy birthday." When I lived in Aspen, I worked for Gracie a few times as she owned a catering business. We called Gracie, who was in a beach town in northern California. We talked about what she was doing and what I was doing, dog- and house-sitting. Gracie said, "How about you house-sit for me next winter?" I said I would call her when I returned to Texas, and we could discuss it.

I sent Kenny a sympathy card. I had not talked to him for five years. He texted me his wedding pictures from over 47 years ago. Naturally, he was devastated by his loss. We talked a few times over the phone over the next nine months.

One day, Kenny called me and said: "Hey, Kathleen. I am here in Florida, playing in the World Senior Tennis Championships. How about jumping on a plane, coming out here, and being my partner?" At that second, I thought he was crazy. I didn't even own a racquet and had not played tennis for over 17 years. But just for a second, I thought I would give anything to play tennis again. As quickly as that thought came into my head, I pushed it down and thought, "That will never happen; don't even think about it." And I didn't. Kenny was a big tease and made me laugh. I always liked that about him. Light-hearted and funny.

After three days of visiting Ginny, I traveled to Riverside and spent another three days visiting David, an old friend, and then on to Palm Springs, where I had a dog- and cat-sitting job for two weeks. While I was in Palm Springs, the Indian Wells Tennis Tournament was being held. I decided to go one day, and while sitting on the grass watching a match on the big screen, I started chatting with a lovely lady. After a short time, I learned Pam was from Carbondale, Colorado, and knew Kenny. What a small world. As it turns out, Kenny and I are now good friends with Pam and her husband Ron, who now live in St. George, Utah.

Then it was back to Austin, where I had a seven-month house-sitting job, no animals. This job was good. I continued working with a few clients over the phone and working on myself.

Then, in late December, I was off to Snowmass (around the corner from Aspen) to cat- and house-sit for Gracie.

A few days after arriving, Kenny sent me a text inviting me for lunch at the Maroon Creek Club, where I had once worked 35 years before. The club is now a fantastic high-end tennis and golf club with clay tennis courts inside and outside. We met there and had a lovely lunch. Then I asked him if he had plans for New Year's Eve. He didn't, so we spent the evening together in Aspen, with all its beautiful lights and fireworks. Good friends having a lovely time in below-freezing weather.

Kenny and I met several times in January, doing various things. Then, one day, Kenny suggested that we play tennis. I said, "You know I don't play tennis anymore." But he convinced me it would be fun. It was worse than I expected. Even though I had kept active walking every day, that was nothing like moving all over the court chasing a ball. And especially moving backward, it felt awkward. It was hilarious and embarrassing, whiffing the ball and mishitting it everywhere. But at 70 years old, what did I expect? About a week later, Kenny said, "Let's try it again." It was February now. I arrived, and Kenny gave me a tennis racquet and bag. It wasn't a big deal because Kenny had several rackets in the garage. But later on, I found out that his daughter said the gift he gave me was like two dozen roses, and she was right. A racquet represented a slim chance that I could play tennis again.

Luckily, after retiring from his painting company, Kenny was a part-time tennis pro who could guide me back to the basics. I was so happy to be on the court again, but I knew it would be long before I felt comfortable moving in every direction. I was also worried about my lack of fitness. Walking every day is a far cry from running around a tennis court.

Kenny and I had dinner several times in February and attended one event. Kenny often talked about his wife, Carolyn, and shared things they did. One night, February 24, 2018, Kenny brought some music with him and played it. He said Carolyn, and he had planned this song for their 50th Wedding Anniversary. They had been married for 47 years when she passed away. Kenny kept talking about Carolyn until I had it! I was tired of being a recovery friend to Kenny. I said: "Kenny, do you know how hurtful it is for you to be constantly talking about Carolyn?" He thought for a moment and said, "No." I asked him, "Do you like me?" He said, "Yes." And like a junior high school girl, I asked: "Do you want to be my boyfriend?" He stalled for a few minutes like I had asked him to define gravity. And finally, he said, "Yes." Then I asked Kenny: "Do you want me to be your girlfriend?" Again, the wheels in his brain turned slowly, and he finally said, "Yes." It was settled; we were in a relationship. We stayed up all night talking, snuggling, and laughing. And for the first time, we kissed.

The next day, Kenny told all his tennis buddies that he had a girlfriend, and they all said: "Wow, are you just finding out?" And they laughed.

I was finally healthy enough to ask tough questions without expectations or attachments. I just wanted to know where I stood. It didn't matter if Kenny said, "No, I don't want to be in a relationship with you." I finally felt safe knowing the truth and feeling good about myself, no matter how he responded.

When a person does not feel safe having healthy boundaries, and they don't feel safe saying "no," there are probably many associated sabotaging beliefs that need to be cleared. For example, a person must feel okay with being rejected, being alone, and the possibility of others getting angry, yelling, judging, making up lies about them, or being thrown out of the family. If you have any of these fears, you probably won't have the courage to say "no" and tell the truth.

From then on, Kenny and I started playing tennis three times a week. Without a doubt, I know Kenny and I were divinely guided to reconnect in perfect timing. If I had not visited Ginny in Laguna Beach on the exact weekend I did, we would not have called Gracie to wish her a Happy Birthday, and I would never have gone to Snowmass. The Universe had conspired to bring us together.

After Gracie returned home at the end of March, her downstairs studio apartment became vacant, and I rented it for a month. At the end of this time, she requested a four-month commitment, and I started thinking about leaving and going back to Houston. Then, to my surprise, Kenny asked me to move in and live with him. He must have known I might need to leave and go to another house-sitting job.

I moved in with Kenny in May 2018. It was a pretty smooth transition, and we played tennis all summer.

I traveled to Sedona in September to take a three-day GeoLove Healing Class. When I returned, it was my 71st birthday. Kenny had bought me golf clubs, baked a cake, made dinner, and made a cute card. Kenny wanted us to learn how to play golf so when we visited friends around the country, we could play golf with them.

We attended the World Senior Games in St. George, Utah, in October. We won a gold medal in mixed doubles, 70s – 74s, and Kenny won the singles.

Regarding golf, I had not played except in a college class. But, if it was outside and some kind of sport, I was all for it. We watched training videos on YouTube and signed up for an online golf instruction program. We practiced, but it did not come easy. Golf is a challenging game to learn, especially when you are 71. In December, we went to Phoenix in our 24' RV and stayed in a park. One day, Kenny said, "I have a surprise for you." After 15 minutes of driving in the car, I told him: "As long as your surprise doesn't have anything to do with golf, I'll be happy." Around the corner, I saw the vast nets from Topgolf. We laughed; Kenny only had one thing on his mind: playing games and competing. And that worked for me most of the time. And when it didn't, I would do my thing, usually working with a client over the phone or on my healing program to get faster results.

We also played in Palm Springs and Phoenix tennis tournaments in the winter. Again, Kenny did well in singles.

When we played golf with some of Kenny's friends in Tuscan, Arizona, I had only played for about five months. I was nervous because I didn't know where my ball would fly or if I could get it off the ground. But I managed not to embarrass myself too much.

The following year, we played in a tennis tournament in Grand Junction in early May. On Saturday night, Kenny and I went out to dinner. Sitting in a quiet corner, Kenny pushed a small card over to me. I opened the envelope and read the sweetest card, asking me to marry him.

I sat there staring at the card without speaking. No one had ever proposed to me in my 71 years. Finally, I said, "Yes." It was a memorable evening. The next day, we went to the mall and visited several jewelry stores looking at rings. I always wanted a simple gold band. We got prices ranging from $600 - $1,200.

Then we went to Starbucks to have a "kick-in-the-pants" coffee drink, as we called it, and Kenny got a brainy idea. He said, "Let's see if Amazon carries gold bands." So, we looked it up and found just what we wanted: two gold bands, $300 each. So, we ordered them.

Seven weeks later, on June 15, 2019, we were married. I didn't have any money, and I didn't want Kenny to have to spend thousands of dollars, so we got married in a beautiful field with Mount Sopris in the background. Only seven of us, Kenny's daughter Jennifer and son-in-law, Tony, who lived nearby; Bill, who did the ceremony, and his partner, Barbara; and good friends Sally, Ray, and Ginny. It was simple, beautiful, and meaningful. No drama. I didn't invite any family members, which worried me greatly, but it turned out okay. We had dinner at the River Valley Ranch Restaurant. Kenny made the cake, and his daughter Jennifer did the beautiful flowers. We spent our honeymoon night at the Historic Colorado Hotel in Glenwood Springs. The next day, we played golf with Ray and Sally. The entire weekend was very enjoyable, loving, and completely drama-free.

That August, we played in Denver's USTA National Husband and Wife Indoor Tennis Championships. Kenny was an excellent player, and I was an intermediate player. We placed 3rd in the combined age division of 140. We won a national silver ball. I didn't know what a big deal it was at the time. Later, a friend of Kenny's who collects tennis memorabilia said if I ever got hard up financially, he would buy the silver ball from me. That was when I knew it was something special. I realized most tennis players who compete their entire lives don't win a National USTA Ball. It's a big deal.

In the winter of 2021-22, we stayed at the over-fifty Palm Creek RV Park in Casa Grande. It has eight tennis courts, 32 pickleball courts, and an excellent 18-hole, par three golf course. It's like being at a summer camp for seniors who want to play all day.

Over the years, many people had asked us if we played pickleball, but Kenny always said, "No, we are too young." One day, after playing tennis with a couple, they said they couldn't play another set because they had a pickleball match lined up. Kenny and I asked, "Doesn't pickleball mess up your tennis?" They said, "No, in fact, the opposite." The next day, we learned the rules and basics. We hit for an hour or so, and we were hooked. We started playing at the local pickleball courts when we returned home to Carbondale, Colorado.

In September, we played in our first Pickleball Tournament in Salida, CO. We didn't win anything but had loads of fun.

So now we have three sports we enjoy, and every day we play one of them – tennis, pickleball, or golf. And sometimes we go for a bike ride. In the winter, Kenny still skis, and I go occasionally. In 2022, at the World Senior Games, Utah, we won gold in the mixed doubles tennis, I won a silver in women's doubles, a gold in the golf handicap, and Kenny won a bronze in the longest drive and a bronze in the pitching competition. These competitions were all in our age group, 75 – 79.

In the winter of 2022-23, we won one gold ball in the Husband-wife National Hardcourts Tennis Championships, two National Championships (silver balls, runner-up) in the Grass Court Championships, and one silver in the 75 - 79 National Tennis Hardcourt Championships. We were thrilled to come home that winter with four National balls each.

November 2022, USTA National Husband-Wife Hardcourt Championships, Claremont, CA. We won Gold first place—combined age group 150 and over.

Huntsman World Senior Games, St George, UT, October 2023

Won 2 gold in tennis (mixed and women's doubles)

Won 1 silver in golf (longest drive)

Won 2 gold in pickleball (singles and mixed)

Won 1 bronze in pickleball (women's doubles)

March 2023 USTA National Husband-Wife Grasscourt Championships, Palms Springs We won a Silver Ball, second place -- combined age group 150 and over.

February 2023 USTA National Mixed Doubles Championships, Palm Springs. We won a Silver Ball, second place – age group 75 – 79.

Our trophy case at home.

Chapter Four

What I Wish I Knew Sooner

For as long as I can remember, I have wanted to help people. I did help people, but I didn't do it with proper discernment and without self-sacrifice. Many other things happened in my life where I put myself in a position to be taken advantage of, and often people did. The result was I felt hurt and resentful. I now take responsibility for all that happened.

Here is a Summary of the classes and courses I took:

In my late 20s, I took the EST Training, a relationship class, and worked with a therapist. I learned we create beliefs and strategies to try and get the attention we so deeply want as youngsters. And then, we continue using these strategies as adults even though they usually don't work well.

In my 30s, I attended the Lighten Up Class three times, worked with an EMDR (Eye Movement Desensitization and Reprocessing) practitioner, and had Network Chiropractor sessions. I took classes in self-esteem and spirituality. I slowly was inching my way up the conscious ladder to feel better about myself.

In my 40s, I attended a Sexual Abuse Group Class; I took all of Landmark Education Classes and most of their Seminars. I took the six-month Introduction to Forum Leaders Course and the year-long Wisdom course. I spent the next year coaching the participants.

In my 50s, I learned and practiced EFT (Emotional Freedom Technique); I took the Yuen Method Training, Wavemaker Coaching, and Tom Stone's year-long class (twice).

In my 60s, I took Matrix Energetics, Seven ThetaHealing® classes (Basic, Advanced, Relationship, Optimal Weight, Intuitive Anatomy, and Intuitive Anatomy Instructors Course, a three-week course) where I had to travel to Idaho and Montana and Calling in the One Certification.

Between each decade, I took dozens of classes in personal development, self-esteem, and spirituality.

Over the past 45 years, I added up the cost and time of the tens of dozens of classes I took, seminars, courses, study and practice sessions, therapy, coaching, medical and healing practitioners, trainings, certifications, marketing, and travel expenses; I believe it was around $200,000. I invested over 20,800 hours, divided by 40 hours a week, divided by 52 weeks a year; it comes out to be about ten years of my life that I devoted to my physical and emotional healing, coaching and healing capabilities, and learning how to market my services.

When I taught ThetaHealing® classes, I provided my students with additional important information that I had learned over the past 30 years so they could transform their lives and their clients' lives faster. Every time I learned something new, I would write it down and put it in a folder until I had lots of critical information to help my clients heal faster. Every client became a personal project of mine. I spent more and more time before a session muscle-checking possible limiting beliefs that were optimal to clear. I practiced this system on myself for years also. So, when I have a session with a client, I already have 8 - 10 limiting beliefs written down that are optimal to clear so my client can reach their goals faster. This was the development of my Holistic Emotional Makeover Success System™ (HEMSS).

My HEMSS became so powerful that my clients often get all ten goals in 12 sessions, plus much more.

When I was 70, I cleared the last significant sabotaging belief regarding romantic relationships, and that was: "I need to chase love to survive." **At that moment, I was**

no longer needy in relationships, and that is when I connected with my husband, Kenny.

What makes my Holistic Emotional Makeover Success System™ such a powerful program is that I thoroughly understand how to quickly identify sabotaging conscious and unconscious beliefs blocking my clients from having what they want. Also, I know human behavior and can dig swiftly and efficiently to discover the root sabotaging beliefs causing the client's problems.

After learning many healing techniques, going through many coaching programs, working with many coaches and therapists, and going to over 100 classes and seminars, I believe that the Holistic Emotional Makeover Success System™ is one of the most potent healing programs in the world. It is unlike any other I know of.

In one to three sessions, several clients with emotional eating problems were relieved of their sabotaging habits. In the first or second session, many clients who had been going to therapy for years said we had identified the abusive incident that had caused them problems for decades.

With the HEMSS, I am now living a magical life! My health is good; I am married to an incredibly fun and kind man. I am playing competitive tennis again after a 17-year layoff, and my husband and I play golf and pickleball. I am so blessed! On top of all this, I transform my clients' lives; what could be more gratifying?

My challenges from the past are now my assets in helping others. Overcoming my challenges, combined with all I have learned -- I now have a unique ability to help and teach others. Plus, I have a deep sense of understanding, compassion, and empathy for my clients as I do for myself.

Climbing up the Conscious Ladder is a process, not a destination. Forty years ago, I was at the bottom of the ladder, filled with insecurities, fear, guilt, and shame. As I have mentioned, according to the late Dr. David Hawkins, people only travel up the ladder an average of five points in a lifetime. Because of my constant search for feeling good about myself and my life, I have traveled up the ladder hundreds of points. And even though I feel good about myself, I still work on myself when something comes up. I have spent at least $200,000 on my personal development over the decades and have no regrets. I now have a magical life filled with good health, love, joy, synchronicity, and contribution.

Every birthday from 30 until 70, I wished to be emotionally healthy before I blew out my candles on the cake. When I reached my 70th birthday, I thought, wow, I guess I have arrived, and I now feel emotionally healthy and deeply grateful. When I say that, it does not mean I am experiencing constant bliss. It means that 99% of the time, I feel thankful, healthy, happy, and at peace. And if something does come up, I can identify and clear the sabotaging beliefs and emotions operating.

My specialty is helping clients raised by angry, controlling, unavailable, or abusive parent(s). However, I have worked successfully with clients who say they had wonderful parents and upbringing.

If you have deep anger towards someone, forgiving them while establishing firm, healthy boundaries is healthy. If the person is toxic and you don't have firm, healthy boundaries, they could easily hurt you repeatedly. When you forgive someone for hurting you, you can love them without the need to spend time with them. However, once you have cleared the beliefs that prevent you from having healthy boundaries, you may choose to have these people in your life in a limited capacity.

Perhaps you have tried many programs without getting your desired results, as I did. And maybe you are still searching. If you are, I think your search is over. And just in case you have any doubt, I offer a Satisfaction Guarantee that will be explained later in the book.

One of my clients had experienced anxiety for seven years. When I asked her what had happened seven years earlier, she thought for a while and said surprisingly, "I had a fight with my sister." At a family gathering, the client's sister said something negative about her husband that was very hurtful and embarrassing. Since that time, they had not communicated. We cleared my client's anger, resentment, betrayal, disappointment, and sadness about this incident. After our session, my client felt neutral about the incident. Two days later, I received an email from my client that said her sister had called and asked if she could come for a visit. When my client's anger and anxiety were cleared, her sister energetically received the new energy of acceptance and caring. When people change their beliefs and emotions, their energy changes, and others often treat them differently.

Life Learning Point:

Under every problem are sabotaging beliefs and unwanted emotions. When they are identified and cleared, the challenge is gone. That is the premise of the Holistic Emotional Makeover Success System™. It is clearing out the sabotaging beliefs that cause you emotional pain and problems and downloading empowering beliefs that bring you safety, peace, and joy.

***

My HEMSS differs from anything out there. I have identified several sabotaging beliefs that must be addressed for fast healing. First, people must feel safe feeling all their emotions and know how to process the unwanted ones. Secondly, they must feel safe being able to see, know, and understand the truth about their childhood, parents, and themselves. Thirdly, they must feel safe around angry people. If you don't have these foundational beliefs, healing can take years or decades, if at all.

There are foundational sabotaging beliefs that must be cleared before healing can occur. A few familiar to healers are: “I don’t deserve a healing,” “I am not worthy of a healing," and "I don't believe my beliefs can be changed instantaneously."

As I worked with hundreds of clients, students, and myself, whenever I discovered a new sabotaging belief or distinction, I wrote it down in my folder, and the HEMSS became more powerful.

I make sure that my clients are "off" for sabotaging beliefs many they don't even know they have, such as "Life is a struggle," "I can't have what I want," "I am not good enough," "It's not safe to be healthy," and "It's not safe to be self-empowered." I also make sure my clients are "on" for empowering beliefs like "I am good enough," "I am worthy," "I have the confidence and capabilities I need to accomplish my goals," and "It is safe for me to be healthy and self-empowered."

It is critical for a healing practitioner to muscle test accurately. Using muscle testing, a practitioner can identify a client's sabotaging beliefs. This can be done over the phone or Zoom thousands of miles away because everything is energy. This is important because some sabotaging beliefs can be unconscious and irrational.

One traumatic childhood incident can shape the rest of a person's life. A child's brain is in the process of developing until their early 20s. Until 8, 9, or 10 years of age, anytime something happens that is upsetting to them or the people around them, a child thinks it is their fault. The reason for this is that they have not yet distinguished themselves as being a separate person from their mother. Until then, the whole world revolves around them. So, when a child has a traumatic experience, they create sabotaging beliefs that often become their programming for life.

Our lives flow magically when we are "on" for empowering beliefs and "off" for limiting beliefs. Nothing stands in the way of our intentions and good health because our new, positive beliefs radiate positive energy, and like attracts like. That's the Law of Attraction—as real as gravity.

My clients experience exceptional personal growth in as little as three to six months, which might take years or decades through other methods. Many of my clients have considered their near-instantaneous mental, emotional, and physical results to be nothing short of miraculous!

Over the past two years, I have noticed that my clients' lives are being transformed faster, achieving their ten goals at lightning speed. It seems incredible even to me.

I want to teach healers, coaches, wellness practitioners, and anyone else who desires to be a leader in emotional health and wellness what I have learned over the past 35 years. I believe that the HEMSS will revolutionize emotional healing worldwide.

Learn how I'm achieving that goal at. In my HEMSS Certification Training, I will teach a step-by-step transformation-proven success system I have developed over the past 35 years. You will receive the Omega Protocol that describes precisely what to do in every challenge. You will take a fellow student through the HEMSS, and a fellow student will take you through the HEMSS so that each student will receive massive clearings and practical experience. There will be weekly training videos. An assistant coach/healer will lead a weekly small group call to provide continuous support and accountability. This training is designed for healers, coaches, and wellness practitioners who want to be leaders in the field of emotional healing. Others interested in learning a powerful system to get more and faster results for their clients are welcome. An application is required.

> "To heal overwhelm, relationships, career, and health challenges, you must find a professional who can identify and clear conscious and unconscious sabotaging "belief programming" and unwanted emotions associated with childhood trauma and negative conditioning. This is the focus of Kathleen's unique step-by-step transformation-proven Holistic Emotional Makeover Success System™ so people can

live happy, healthy, and successful lives easily and quickly."

– Kathleen Fors

Chapter Five

Testimonials From HEMSS Clients

Kathleen's Holistic Emotional Makeover Success System™ and her CORE technique are nothing short of life-changing and amazing! If you are looking for a deep understanding of yourself, why you do what you do, and feel how you feel, as well as how past trauma (big and small) has shaped and controlled you, look no further. Kathleen has an amazing ability to ask the right discovery questions, really listen, and then use her approach to fully surface and clear previous and probably buried but unresolved trauma (pains, hurts, disappointments, resentments, fears, and more). I have tried numerous approaches, courses, books, teachers, counselors...you name it! Nothing has come close. After our consultation, we listed ten goals for me. However, after the first session, we added five more. By the time we had completed Kathleen's 12-session package, I had reached all of my 15 goals and experienced numerous more wins that I was not even aware of.

My relationships with my stepchildren, which were previously strained, are now better than ever. Honest communication between my husband and me has improved. Other important relationships that were suffering are now good again, and I am being nurtured. I feel totally self-empowered in the best way possible, and I am thoroughly enjoying my life, which has totally changed.

If you desire to improve your life in any way, don't wait any longer to give the Holistic Emotional Makeover Success System™ a serious look and have a consultation. You won't regret it.

L.S., Colorado

***

Kathleen Fors is an exceptional Mental Health and Wellness Coach and human being. To work with her has truly been a blessing. After twelve sessions with Kathleen, I have made grand, transformative changes. Despite being doubtful initially, I can wholeheartedly say that the Holistic Emotional Makeover Success System is akin to a miracle. In trusting her and the process, I've healed old wounds and developed into a version of myself I didn't even know was possible. With Kathleen's thoughtfulness, honesty, and grace, I've broken down past beliefs stored in my body and rebuilt myself into a person who aligns with who I really am and who I want to be. My potential continues to mushroom due to the work with Kathleen Fors. I truly recommend this experience for anybody who wants to heal from their past, savor their present, and flourish in their future. Thank you. Thank you. Thank you, Kathleen. Your guidance is the greatest gift. People like you come along once in a lifetime. There is just a thank you to say and more thank you.

D.S., Florida

***

I have been a licensed psychotherapist for 25 years in private practice and have trained, supervised, and employed many therapists. Kathleen works best with her clients and gets better results than anyone I have seen. Working with Kathleen, I stopped emotionally overeating and lost 25 pounds in 3 months. The rest of my life improved drastically, too! I am overjoyed.

C.P., Texas

***

My experience working with Kathleen has been life-changing. I was going through a tough time in my life when I first connected with her.

My husband's best friend died, which was devastating and affected him mentally, and he became challenging to live with. We have a small business together, and due to his emotional challenges, I worked 80 hours a week, trying to keep it going and fulfilling my customer's needs. Covid hit, and things got worse.

My marriage was falling apart; we were oddly even busier than ever, and I was exhausted, humiliated, and falling apart emotionally and physically. I could hardly eat, never left my house, and stopped doing anything besides working.

My friends begged me to reach out to someone. So, I searched for a therapist and spoke to many on the phone. None of which I found any confidence in or connection with.

One day, out of nowhere, I found Kathleen Fors online in my Google search. We spoke, she told me about her program, and I committed to what would be a life-changing experience. One that saved my marriage, business, and, most importantly, myself.

Kathleen is an angel that was sent to me. She has guided me through so many struggles while guiding me to my own self-awareness.

The journey with Kathleen is one that every single person would benefit from, and I encourage everyone to commit to her program.

Kathleen will not tell you what to do or how to do it. Her practice and special talents make you, as yourself, come to your realization. Things that are right in front of you that could never be recognized without her guidance.

Since my sessions with Kathleen, my business has grown with more employees, and I got back to who I am - a fantastic woman with many talents, accomplishments, and a transformed marriage.

I honestly don't know where I would be or if I would be here to write this if I had not met Kathleen. She is a gift from God, Mother Nature, or a star placed on Earth to help others.

T.L., California

Chapter Six

Next Steps

If you have a weight problem, for example, I can understand. Ninety-seven percent of all people who go on diets, including the participants on the hit show "The Biggest Loser," fail to keep the weight off for longer than a year, even though those who do succeed face a never-ending battle, forever challenged with a lifetime of counting calories, excessive exercise or stressful discipline.

Most people can temporarily manage unwanted behavior through sheer willpower; however, not only is this painful and exhausting, but it usually doesn't work over the long term. This is what happens when people try to manage their behavior. Instead, changing their "belief programming" is a much more efficient and effective way to change behavior without straining.

If other programs have failed you, it's not because something is wrong with you; you just need a new and different approach. And it's changing your "belief system programming" instead of trying to manage your behavior. That is what the Holistic Emotional Makeover Success System™ is all about. The ultimate proven success system, 100% Satisfaction Guaranteed.

Is This You?

Read the statements below to determine whether the Holistic Emotional Makeover Success System™ is right for you.

- **I feel unsuccessful.** Despite extensive personal development classes, coaching, books, and counseling, I feel blocked or stuck.

- **I am stuck in negative feelings.** I suffer from

stress, anger, overwhelm, anxiety, depression, sabotaging behaviors, and irrational fears.

- **Something just *feels* off.** Despite appearing successful to others, on the inside, I feel frustrated, unhappy, or feel like something is missing.

- **I often ask myself, "What am I doing wrong?"** Even though I lead a healthy lifestyle, I suffer from health challenges.

- **I have challenges with food.** I experience emotional eating, eating disorders, and unhealthy eating habits or have problems with my weight.

- **I am so tired!** I suffer from chronic fatigue and want more energy.

- **I can't sleep.** I have trouble sleeping and don't know why. Nothing seems to help.

- **I am overwhelmed.** I often feel overwhelmed by

life and have difficulty making decisions.

- **People seem to take advantage of me.** I am easily intimidated or manipulated by others and find it hard to stand up for myself.

- **I am a "workaholic."** I work too much, often at the expense of other aspects of my life (friends, family, health, etc.).

- **I am unsuccessful in creating and sustaining a healthy, loving relationship.** I don't understand how relationships work and what behaviors are sabotaging them.

- **My emotions are ruling my life.** I am either completely controlled by my emotions, or I do things to avoid dealing with them and try to numb them.

- **I am afraid of my success.** I am committed to my achievement, but I still fear being successful and self-empowered.

- **I put important things off.** I know what I need to be doing but often wait until the last minute to get things done. I procrastinate.

- **I am in a rut.** I know I am competent, but I am in a professional slump and want to get out of it.

- **I sometimes feel angry, resentful, fearful, embarrassed, guilty, or shameful toward myself or others.**

- **I carry the weight of the world on my shoulders.** I find myself shouldering other people's problems at my own expense and often have trouble saying "no."

- **I have been through a major life change.** I want to go through this transition skillfully and successfully. (Big changes might include marriage/divorce, death, children, job change, financial issues, etc.)

- **My marriage is on the rocks.** It feels unstable or stagnant, and I want to feel in love again and have my relationship work.
- **I suffered negative childhood experiences.** As a child, my parents or guardians were abusive or negligent.
- **I'm afraid my issues may be hurting my children.** I am concerned that I am passing down unwanted habits and conditioning to my children and want to know how to avoid doing so.
- **I don't like being around other people for any length of time.** I experience social anxiety, and I am uncomfortable in social situations.
- **I feel insecure.** I know I am not being authentic, and I want to be comfortable and confident with who I am.

- **I want to be completely free from addiction.** I am in recovery from substance abuse (clean and sober for at least 90 days), and I want to resolve the core issue that caused my addiction.

- **I feel aimless, purposeless.** I don't feel I am doing what I am supposed to be doing. I want to discover and live my true purpose.

- **I feel limited and stuck by my situation.** I want to feel good about myself and my life regardless of circumstances.

Another way to check if the HEMSS is right for you is to go down the list. I have worked successfully with clients who experienced these problems:

- Abuse/Trauma as a Child, adolescent, and Adult.

- Accident recovery.

- ADD/ADHD, focus and concentration challenges.

- Addictions, except drugs and alcohol, unless living in a treatment center.
- Anger Issues.
- Anxiety.
- Athletic performance issues.
- Autoimmune conditions.
- Boundary issues, unable to say "no."
- Career slump/Professional dislike.
- Change of life/Mid-life challenges.
- Chronic fatigue syndrome.
- Codependent behavior.
- Communication problems.
- Death or loss of a parent, spouse, child, friend, or pet.

- Depression.
- Divorce aftermath.
- Eating disorders.
- Emotional pain.
- Fear of success and failure.
- Feeling stuck, in a rut, or blocked.
- Health problems, a wide range.
- High blood pressure.
- Insecurity/Discomfort around others/Social anxiety.
- Lack of motivation.
- Major life transitions.
- Marital problems.
- Over-responsibility.

- Overwhelm.
- Overwork/Workaholism/Over-commitment.
- Phobias.
- Polymyalgia Rheumatica or other inflammation conditions.
- Procrastination.
- Recurrent or chronic infections.
- Relationship/Dating issues.
- Self-expression challenges.
- Stalled career/Purposeless.
- Stress.
- Successful, yet feels something is missing.
- Victim mentality and behavior.
- Weight loss.

Past clients and students I have worked with include coaches, healers, therapists, speakers, authors, small business owners, CEOs, managers, students, and homemakers.

Requirements to go through the HEMSS or take the HEMSS Training:

If you want to participate in one of my programs, you must have the following qualities:

- You must be coachable.
- You must keep your agreements and appointments.
- You must be honest and willing to share information about your childhood traumas, including sexual abuse.
- You must be willing to take responsibility for your part in all of your adult challenges.
- The investment in one of my programs must be

without financial hardship and stress.

(Note: If you have a drug or alcohol addiction, you must first be in an on-site rehab program.)

***

My HEMSS has a "Satisfaction Guarantee." After the second session, if a person does not experience a shift, they can discontinue, and all unused fees will be returned. No other program I have ever taken (tens of dozens), and no other program I know of, provides this type of guarantee. My success rate working with clients is 97%. Those few I could not help refused to take responsibility for their behavior and insisted on blaming their parent(s) for their problems.

Visit https://www.kathleenfors.com/callkathleen to schedule an Empowerment Consultation. We will discuss your biggest challenges and develop a list of 10 goals. Then, I will share the details of the HEMSS

and why it is so effective and fast, and I will further explain the Satisfaction Guarantee. And if we both feel we are a good fit, we can work together.

If you are a healer, coach, or wellness practitioner and want to get more and faster results for your clients, or if you want to be in the wellness field, strongly consider Kathleen's HEMSS Online Certified Training Program. www.KathleenFors.com/HEMSSTraining. In the HEMSS Online Certified Training, I will teach everything I have learned over the past 35 years. You will receive the Omega Protocol that describes what to do in every challenge. You will take a fellow student through the HEMSS, and a fellow student will take you through the HEMSS so that each student will receive massive clearings. An assistant coach/healer will provide weekly support and accountability, leading a small group call. There will also be weekly training videos. This training is designed for healers, coaches, and wellness practitioners. Others interested in learning a powerful system to transform people's lives are also welcome. An application is required.

Chapter Seven

Resources

If you are considering working with a healer, coach, or therapist, here are some questions you may want to ask:

- What is your specialty if you have one?
- Do you have a system or program for healing my challenges?
- Do you use muscle testing/checking?
- Do you use an alternative healing technique to clear sabotaging beliefs and emotions? And if so, what type of technique?

- Can you teach me how to process unwanted emotions when they come up?
- How many sessions, on average, do you work with a client to achieve their top 10 goals?
- What is your success rate?
- Do you have a satisfaction guarantee?
- Can you work over the phone or Zoom if I choose to do so?

Important foundation beliefs for a good and lasting relationship:

- I feel whole and complete with or without a partner.
- It is safe for me to see, know, and understand the truth about a person when I get to know them initially, without ignoring or sweeping red flags

under the rug.

- I have healthy boundaries, and I can say "no" easily.
- I feel safe making a request without expectations.
- I use conscious language when communicating, using "I" instead of "you."
- I feel comfortable communicating with my partner if they do something that feels disrespectful.
- I am safe being introspective and recognize my part in an upset or disagreement between my partner and me.
- I feel whole and complete even if I get rejected.
- I feel safe being alone.
- I know what values are important to me.

- My important values match up with my partner's.
- I am free of needs regarding my partner.
- My lifestyle matches up with my partner, or they complement each other.
- My partner and I understand and agree on who is responsible for household duties.
- My partner and I have a mutual understanding regarding earning, saving, and spending money.
- If we decide to have children, my partner and I have mutual child-raising philosophies.
- I am open and willing to get help if our relationship has challenges.

Foundation beliefs for being and feeling whole & complete.

- I feel safe, whole, and complete without anything missing.
- I am safe feeling all of my emotions.
- I know how to process unwanted emotions.
- I feel safe and comfortable expressing myself.
- I feel okay around angry people with appropriate discernment.
- I am present and authentic.
- I trust and act on my intuition.
- I feel self-loving and accept myself.
- I feel safe and secure being introspective and take responsibility for my part in an upset.
- I can communicate authentically without an

agenda.

- I have healthy boundaries, and I feel safe saying "no."
- I am honest and can share appropriate feelings and opinions without judgment and fear. I use conscious language.
- I feel comfortable with change and the unknown.
- I am self-sufficient.
- I know how to protect myself.
- My heart and mind are open to other people.
- I take action from clarity.
- I respond instead of reacting.
- I can see and understand the truth about my childhood and my parents without feeling bad.
- I let go and allow without trying to control things

or force an outcome.

- I trust myself and make good decisions.
- I am content right now wherever I am, physically, emotionally, and financially, while still moving forward in my life.
- I am living my purpose.
- I feel safe and cared for by the "Creator of All That Is."

***

To receive your Free Copy of *"How to Learn the Single Most Powerful Tool for Transforming Your Life,"* a comprehensive report on why feeling your emotions is critical and how to process them, go to my site at https://www.kathleenfors.com/core

***

Here is a summary of the classes, programs, training, and certifications I have taken over the past 45 years. The length of each one ranges from three days to one year.

- EST Training, Sacramento.
- Relationship Class, San Francisco.
- Lighten-up, Santa Barbara.
- Dozens of Classes at the Santa Barbara Adult Education School include Self-esteem, personal growth, spirituality, health, and communication.
- Money Coaching, Santa Barbara.
- Warrior, Los Angeles.
- Spiritual Classes from private individuals, Santa Barbara, Austin.

- Landmark Education Curriculum. All events occurred in the Los Angeles area, except Seminars held in Santa Barbara, Chico.
    - Basic Forum.
    - Advanced Forum.
    - Communication Course.
    - Wisdom Course.
    - Introduction to the Forum Leaders Program.
    - Seminars, Santa Barbara.
- The Yuen Method, Santa Barbara.
- Attended Coach University online.
- Hudson Institute, Santa Barbara.
- Accountability Coaching, Santa Barbara.
- Emotional Freedom Technique #1 & #2 (EFT),

Los Angeles.

- Emotional Freedom Technique Intensive, Maui.
- Spiritual Coaching, New Jersey.
- Great Life Technologies year-long class, twice, virtual.
- WaveMaker Coaching, San Diego.
- "The Twelve Causes of Human Problems," San Diego.
- Sales class (2), San Diego, San Francisco.
- Heart Selling, San Jose.
- Tantra Class, Santa Barbara.
- Tom Stone Coaching, virtual.
- Wavemaker Coaching, Certified Wavemaker Coach, San Diego.

- Matrix Energetics, Canada.
- Calling in the One, Certified Coach, Los Angeles.
- How to Talk to Men, Austin.
- Reiki level one, Austin.
- The Akashic Records, Austin.
- ThetaHealing® Institute of Knowledge. Most classes held in Idaho and Montana.
    - Basic.
    - Advanced.
    - DNA 3
    - Soul Mate.
    - Optimal Weight.
    - Abundance.
    - Manifestation.

  - Intuitive Anatomy.
  - Basic and Advanced Certified Instructor's Course.
  - Intuitive Anatomy Certified Instructor's Course.
- GeoLove Healing, Sedona.
- Prosperity Classes, San Diego.
- Marketing Classes (7), Los Angeles, San Francisco, Austin, San Diego, San Jose, and the rest online.
- Attended Spiritual Groups, Santa Barbara, Austin, Houston.

Over the years, besides all my classes, I worked individually with nine different coaches, eight healers, four therapists and learned four healing modalities.

Chapter Eight

Acknowledgements

Thank you to my sister Beverly and her husband, John Downey, for your unconditional love and extensive support. You were always there when I needed help. Thank you to Beverly for caring for our mother for eight and a half years in assisted living homes, visiting her weekly.

Thank you, sister Shirley Weldon, for your love and support.

Thank you to Candace White for your friendship and continuous support when I lived in Santa Barbara.

Thank you to Faustina Washburn for your friendship and financial support when it was desperately needed.

Thank you to the late Thomas Leonard, founder of CoachU and Coachville.

Thank you to Vianna Stibal for ThetaHealing®.

Thank you to Tom Stone for "The Twelve Causes of Human Problems" and "Pure Awareness Techniques."

Thank you to Dr. Kam Yuen for "The Yuen Method."

Thank you to Robert F. Kennedy Jr. and "Children's Health Defense.org" for your dedication to protecting children's health and sharing the truth.

Thank you to Mike Adams, the Health Ranger for NaturalNews.com, for relentlessly finding and sharing the truth and providing clean organic food.

Thank you to my clients and students; I learned so much from you.

Thank you to Carolyn Choate, who set up my accounts with Amazon and other retailers so this book could be purchased digitally and in paperback from all major booksellers.

Thank you to my dear husband, Kenny Sawer, for your love, support, laughter, and our magical life. Thank you also for returning me to the world of competitive sports I so love!

Thank you to the "Creator of All There Is"; I know I have always been supported.

Chapter Nine

About The Author

Over the past 45 years, Kathleen's primary focus and journey has been healing herself. She took hundreds of classes and got professional help from dozens of healers, coaches, and wellness practitioners. She overcame a 22-year binge eating disorder, a severe 5-year inflammation illness, and victim behavior.

At 76 years young, Kathleen is now living her best, most magical life. Six years ago, she returned to playing tennis after a 17-year hiatus. She is also enjoying a wonderful new marriage (her first) with a remarkable man, who competes as her tournament partner. Kathleen is healthy, fit, self-empowered, happy, and grateful.

Chapter Ten

References

Tom Stone, Pure Awareness Techniques, and "The 12 Causes of Human Problems"; InnerGreatnessGlobal.com

"Feelings Buried Alive Never Die . . .," Karol Truman.

"Messages from the Body;" Dr. Michael Lincoln, Ph.D.

"Power vs. Force;" David Hawkins, M.D., Ph.D.

"The Power of Now," Eckhart Tolle.

ChildrensHealthDefense.org; founder Robert F. Kenney, Jr.

NaturalNews.com; Mike Adams, the Health Ranger.

www.ingramcontent.com/pod-product-compliance
Lightning Source LLC
LaVergne TN
LVHW020718110826
845149LV00012B/2312
* 9 7 9 8 9 8 8 5 6 5 0 8 6 *